Praise for

Living in the spotlight of fulltime ministry can be tough on a marriage, which is why I'm so glad my friends Geoff and Sherry Surratt have written *Together*. With an invaluable his-and-her perspective, this book reveals how to navigate the challenges that come when couples minister together. Their combined wisdom and insight are invaluable for any couple wanting to grow closer to each other even as they grow closer to God.

CHRIS HODGES
Senior Pastor, Church of the Highlands
Author of *Fresh Air* and *The Daniel Dilemma*

Over the years my family has experienced the challenges of ministry firsthand, which is why I am so thankful for Geoff and Sherry Surratt's new book. The powerful, insightful, and real-life illustrations in *Together: A Guide for Couples in Ministry* will serve as a great tool to help other couples navigate the privileges and tests that come with full-time ministry.

CRAIG GROESCHEL
Pastor of Life.Church
Author of *Daily Power: 365 Days of Fuel for Your Soul*

At the risk of sounding obvious, being married and in ministry is tricky! In *Together*, through transparency, humor, and practicality, Sherry and Geoff help us know we are not alone. They are not only great writers, they live out their words with great passion and intentionally. It's really clear they love *and* like each other in the midst of ministry; this book can help you do the same.

TED LOWE
Speaker and Author
Director of MarriedPeople.org at the Rethink Group

Sherry and Geoff Surratt are practitioners and not theoreticians. Their practical wisdom, forged in the crucible of their own ministry and marriage, uniquely qualifies them to speak help and hope to other ministry couples. You will find *Together* a fresh, authentic, and vulnerable work full of pragmatic insight, encouragement, and guidance. Geoff and Sherry invite us to cultivate the relational vibrancy so essential to ministry effectiveness and longevity. Invest in both your ministry and relationship . . . read this book!

HARVEY POWERS, PHD
Licensed Clinical Psychologist
Leadership Mentor and Coach
The Redimere Group

The challenges of ministry are numerous! Add to those challenges the desire to build and sustain a happy, healthy, marriage while ministering together, and the degree of difficulty has compounded. In this book my friends Geoff and Sherry Surratt have given ministry couples who are navigating the important journey of ministry and marriage the benefit of their efforts and experience. You can learn from their wisdom and insight as you lessen the degree of difficulty for your marriage and minister together. This is a must read for every ministry couple!

TOM LANE
Lead Executive Senior Pastor/Dallas Campus Pastor
Gateway Church

Whenever I get to talk to Geoff and Sherry Surratt, coauthors of *Together*, I smile, laugh, and go away encouraged. The same thing happened when I read this book. It's not only practical but laugh-out-loud funny. I don't care if you are in ministry with your spouse or not, reward yourself by reading this new work about real, live ministry and how to thrive in all the ups and downs.

DAVE TRAVIS
CEO, Leadership Network

Geoff and Sherry Surratt are fun people to be with. Their new book, *Together*, provides an open, honest, and refreshing look at the challenges of marriage and ministry. We recommend this book to all couples involved in serving God together.

STEVE AND DEB TIBBERT
Senior Pastor, King's Church London

Geoff and Sherry Surratt are an outstanding *couple*. Yes, they each have significant ministries in their own right, but it's their thriving togetherness over decades of ministry that I absolutely want to wholeheartedly endorse. This amazing couple have not only survived but thrived through the ups and downs of ministry over the long haul. Their new book, *Together: A Guide for Couples in Ministry*, is a must read for every young ministry couple.

MICHAEL MURPHY
Founding Director, Leaderscape

I love the heart and direction of this book. It is a much-needed guide for navigating the challenge of life in the fishbowl of ministry and marriage.

HERBERT COOPER
Senior Pastor, People's Church

Sometimes within the same organization, and sometimes in separate endeavors, Geoff and Sherry have faced the unique challenges of marriage and vocational ministry all their married life. This articulate and vulnerable sharing of their ministry/marriage journey will be wonderfully helpful and encouraging to other ministry couples.

SIBYL TOWNER
Co-author of *Listen to My Life* (www.onelifemaps.com)
Co-director with husband, Dick, of The Springs Retreat Center
(thespringsindiana.org)

I've seen Geoff and Sherry Surratt navigate the challenges of marriage and ministry through the years, both in roles with start-up churches and national organizations that required them to come up with creative ways to make their family life work. Their journey has taken some unexpected turns, and they've made some daring decisions. I think the experiences they share in *Together* will help any couple during the best of times, the less-than-ideal times, and the many days in the middle that make the real difference for two people together.

REGGIE JOINER
Founder and CEO of Orange and the Rethink Group, Inc.

I was first aware of Geoff's ministry through his hugely important role in helping Seacoast Church become such a successful multi-site model. More recently I've had the privilege of working with him and Sherry as part of the team who have been helping to run the European Learning Communities. They are such a great couple with so much to teach us. Read and be encouraged!

DR. DAVE SMITH
Senior Pastor of Kingsgate Community Church
Peterborough, UK

My family has experienced the challenges of ministry together firsthand, and we've learned over the years how important it is to be intentional in protecting our marriage. Through Geoff and Sherry's wisdom, encouragement, and practical advice, *Together* will help ministry couples do just that.

DR. CHRIS RAILEY
Senior Director of Leadership and Church Development
Assemblies of God

If you are a parent in ministry, you'll want to read *Together*. In this book the Surratts, in their authentic style, will help you navigate the ups and downs of having a thriving family life while doing ministry together.

DAVE FERGUSON
Lead Pastor, Community Christian Church
Author of *Helping People Find Their Way Back to God*
and *Starting Over*

Whether its in an official capacity or not, if you are in ministry and you're married, you have to figure out the "together" part. My family has experienced the challenges firsthand, and there are some pitfalls we never saw coming. We are going to give this book to every family we know, including our kids. Geoff and Sherry are honest about their highs and lows, and that's really the point. Knowing how to identify and anticipate with the Surratt's thirty-plus years of experience will be a huge advantage to you. I wish we'd had this book a long, long time ago.

DR. TIM HARLOW
Senior Pastor
Parkview Christian Church

Together is a much-needed guide for navigating the challenges of life in the fishbowl of ministry and marriage.

BRADY BOYD
Senior Pastor
New Life Church, Colorado Springs
Author of *Addicted to Busy*

It's no mystery that the ministry marriage is a place of great joy, but also great stress. You can multiply that for couples who are in ministry together! In this volume Geoff and Sherry Surratt offer sage and timely advice for those who have embraced the unique challenge of ministry *together*.

MICHAEL FLETCHER
Senior Pastor
Manna Church

Geoff and Sherry have written the book we wish we had had as we started in full-time ministry together forty years ago! You'll love the vulnerability in their stories and the practical questions with each chapter to get you talking.

TOM AND CHAUNDEL HOLLADAY
Teaching Pastor
Saddleback Church

together

together

A GUIDE FOR
COUPLES IN MINISTRY

GEOFF AND SHERRY
SURRATT

THOMAS NELSON
Since 1798

Published in Nashville, Tennessee, by Thomas Nelson. Thomas Nelson is a registered trademark of HarperCollins Christian Publishing.

Thomas Nelson titles may be purchased in bulk for educational, business, fund-raising, or sales promotional use. For information, please e-mail SpecialMarkets@ThomasNelson.com

Unless otherwise noted, Scripture quotations are taken from the Holy Bible, New International Version®, NIV®. Copyright © 1973, 1978, 1984, 2011 by Biblica Inc.™ Used by permission. All rights reserved worldwide.

Scripture quotations marked KJV are taken from the King James Version. Public domain.

Scripture quotations marked NLT are taken from the Holy Bible, New Living Translation, copyright © 1996, 2004, 2007, 2013, 2015 by Tyndale House Foundation. Used by permission of Tyndale House Publishers Inc., Carol Stream, Illinois 60188. All rights reserved.

ISBN 978-0-7180-9590-1 (softcover)
ISBN 978-0-7180-9591-8 (e-book)

Library of Congress Cataloging-in-Publication Data

Surratt, Geoff, 1962- author.
Together : a guide for couples doing ministry together / Geoff and Sherry Surratt.
Nashville : Thomas Nelson, 2018. | Includes bibliographical references.
LCCN 2017027564 | ISBN 9780718095901
LCSH: Missions. | Married people—Religious life.
LCC BV2063 .S96 2018 | DDC 253.086/55—dc23 LC record available
at https://lccn.loc.gov/2017027564

Printed in the United States of America

18 19 20 21 22 23 LSC 6 5 4 3 2 1

*To our kids, Mike and Brittainy: you
know the many, many mistakes we made
raising you, but you love us anyway.*

*And to our daughter-in-law, Hilary, who joined
our crazy family and made us so much better.*

We are so proud of each of you.

*To our grandkids, Maggie, Mollie, and Mason: you
fill our second act with laughter and sunshine.*

About Leadership Network

Leadership Network fosters innovation movements that activate the church to greater impact. We help shape the conversations and practices of pacesetter churches in North America and around the world. The Leadership Network mindset identifies church leaders with forward-thinking ideas and helps them to catalyze those ideas, resulting in movements that shape the church.

Together with HarperCollins Christian Publishing, the biggest name in Christian books, the NEXT imprint of Leadership Network moves ideas to implementation for leaders to take their ideas to form, substance, and reality. Placed in the hands of other church leaders, that reality begins spreading from one leader to the next . . . and to the next . . . and to the next, where that idea begins to flourish into a full-grown movement that creates a real, tangible impact in the world around it.

NEXT: A Leadership Network Resource committed to helping you grow your next idea.

NEXT

LEADERSHIP NETWORK

leadnet.org/NEXT

Contents

Introduction

~

It was August 6, 1982. It was a normal day for St. Louis, Missouri, hot and muggy-humid, with rain predicted for the evening. But it was far from a normal day for me (Sherry). This was my wedding day. My dress hung suspended from a hanger precariously perched over the top of my bedroom door in a cocoon of tissue paper, bedecked with puffed sleeves of lace and pearls, with the hoop skirt (yes, I really wore one) hanging flat on the door behind it. My normally messy room looked like a tornado had blown through, leaving clothes, suitcases, makeup bag, and hair accessories in its wake. The wedding was set for 7:00 p.m.; my nerves were set for overload.

Though early in the day, there were still details to take care of. My aunt Carol, a cake decorator, was doing our three-tier wedding cake, complete with a running water fountain. But she still lacked the customary bride and groom figurines. I ran to pick them up from a florist shop near my house, my hair in humongous plastic rollers affixed with huge bobby pins. Standing at the counter, the man who waited on me observed my head with amusement and asked, "Getting ready for something special?"

My insides did a somersault when I thought of everything that still had to get done. I had to get these rollers out of my hair. Makeup, shoes, the gifts for the bridesmaids; these essentials weren't going to pack themselves. I had to get a move on. As I rushed out the door and into my car to finish packing, I wondered for a brief moment what Geoff was doing. Was he as nervous as I was? Was he thinking about me? I paused for just a second as the thought hit me: *After today I will be living with a man.* It didn't occur to me until later to wonder why I had never really given this much thought during our entire year of being engaged. What was it going to be like to live with a man?

The bride's room at the church was a flurry of dresses, lip gloss, and lots of hair spray. Lots and lots of hair spray. I remember a moment, standing in front of the mirror, critically inspecting my feathered bangs, wondering if my hair had enough "poof." Photographs show that if there were any more poof, my head might have exploded.

There was a moment of panic when we couldn't find Jenny, my one-year-old niece, until we realized she had crawled under my hoops as I stood in front of the mirror. She was happily sucking her thumb. We all made it to the photographer and smiled and said "Cheese" at all the right moments. As the bridesmaids headed back to the dressing room, I was taken to a room off the church foyer. A family friend had volunteered to video Geoff and me separately, to record some special thoughts we could replay later as we remembered this special day. I smiled and giggled and, looking into the camera, I told Geoff several times how much I loved him. He was my best friend. I was thankful God had sent him into my life, and I couldn't wait to get started on our life together.

On my dad's arm I made my way up the stairs to the church auditorium, reminding my dad one more time not to step on my humongous dress. He just nodded and smiled, but I'm sure he was thinking, *You try holding it together while trying not to trip over a huge marshmallow with hoops.* I watched as, one by one, my best friends promenaded down the aisle to the refrains of "How Deep Is Your Love" by the Bee Gees to take their places on the burnt orange–carpeted steps. I remember thinking, *This is it. I'm getting married!*

Thirty-some years later I often think back to that naive young lady who was married on August 6. She didn't have a clue. Her thoughts were consumed with wedding flowers and dresses and new outfits for the honeymoon. She thought about her new life in Houston, Texas, married to a youth pastor, but she had given no thought to what it would be like to live that far from her family for the first time. She didn't know how to cook anything except mac and cheese, had never balanced her own checkbook, and for many years still thought makeup, shoes, and hair accessories were essentials.

While I (Geoff) stood at the front of the church in a rented wide-lapelled tuxedo and awesome mullet, waiting for my beautiful fiancée to come down the aisle, I wasn't thinking about our uncertain future, the challenges of ministry, or the complexity of marriage. I was thinking about the wedding night. When this ceremony was over, we would finally get into a limo and head to the Henry VIII Hotel with a heart-shaped Jacuzzi tub. (It was almost as cheesy as it sounds.) By this time tomorrow, all the hopes and dreams of my twenty years of life would be fulfilled.

Even though I didn't spend much time thinking about our future, I knew we would be fine. I had a new job in Houston, working as a youth pastor for my father. So after the honeymoon we were moving nine hundred miles away from Sherry's friends and family. The job paid twenty thousand dollars a year; I remember wondering what we'd do with all that money. Sherry had just finished her freshman year of college, so she would be a full-time student, work a part-time job, and help me in the youth ministry. What could go wrong?

I don't remember much about the wedding. I remember Sherry looking amazing in her white dress and floppy hat. She sang a Karen Carpenter tune, my request, which was the most beautiful thing I'd ever heard. We plighted troths, "death do us parted," and exchanged rings. The food at the reception looked amazing, but I didn't get a chance to eat any. Finally, we were off on the honeymoon; two barely adults on a vacation alone. We had a blast.

A week later we loaded the few things Sherry owned, hitched her 1974 olive green Dodge Dart to a twenty-foot U-Haul truck, and headed to Houston. A few miles out of town Sherry began to cry. She cried through Missouri, Arkansas, and into Texas. She was nineteen years old and moving hundreds of miles away from home to live with me. No wonder there were tears.

For the first time I started to think about what I'd gotten us into: Sherry was leaving behind everyone she loved, I was going to work for my father, we had no money, and I was going into full-time ministry without a clue. I fought back a few tears of my own on that long ride down Interstate 44. What were we thinking?

All these years later we are still on the long ride of doing ministry and marriage together. We've gained two amazing kids and two beautiful granddaughters and a handsome grandson, and we've lost four grandparents and my mom along the way. We've had four dogs, multiple fish, and a frog named Jumper, who met his maker after jumping in the sewer. We've been youth pastors, children's pastors, schoolteachers, administrators, and consultants. Sherry has been a CEO, and I've been Rick Warren's driver for a day. The journey has been wonderful and awful, scary and fun. There are times ministry is a disaster, and our marriage is on life support, and times ministry is amazing and our marriage sparkles.

Thirty-plus years of marriage and ministry together is a long time. We have learned, and are still learning, a lot along the way, and we have had some incredible experiences. We are amazed we've had opportunities to teach thousands of leaders, meet world leaders, and lead ministries that impact tens of thousands of people. We are very average people whom God uses in spite of ourselves. We are jealous of ministry couples we see on Facebook with perfect churches, perfect kids, and perfect hair. We wish we had their lives, but we don't. We wish it hadn't taken us twenty-five years of marriage before we learned to pray together. We wish we had taken our kids on amazing memory-making trips on their milestone birthdays instead of to dinners at Applebee's. We wish every day was a new experience of spiritual insight and revelation instead of budgets and board meetings. What we are realizing after doing ministry together for so long is that we will never be the Facebook couple, but we can fiercely love each other, our family, and the people we minister to.

Something else we're learning is that there are more ministry couples like us than the perfect couples on Facebook. Most of the couples we talk to struggle with the same questions we do. How do you prioritize your spouse when ministry is all encompassing? How do you raise kids who are seminormal and love Jesus in the fishbowl of ministry? How do you discover whether God is calling you to be faithful or move on when ministry knocks you down? That is why we decided to write this book. We don't pretend to have all the answers to all the difficult questions, but we believe we are learning some important principles along the journey that might help other couples like us.

We don't want this book to read like a how-to manual on marriage and ministry, an old couple telling you how to do it right. The image we have is sitting down together at our favorite Starbucks and talking about the ups and downs of doing marriage and ministry together. We'll be as transparent and authentic as possible. We'll share our mistakes and foibles and the lessons we're learning. We'll talk about the unstated expectations we brought into marriage, the difficulty of raising preacher's kids, and the times when we both thought our marriage was over. We'll discuss the thrill of seeing God use us to change people's eternal destinies and the challenge of working together and working apart. We're not afraid to talk about the hard stuff, and we'll invite you to tackle it too. We admit we struggle with bad attitudes, self-ishness, and sometimes still crumble in the face of criticism. But it's okay. We bet you do too.

We are writing for couples in ministry. You may be a young couple just starting down the road of ministry, and you'd like to not pay the same "dumb tax" we paid. You may be in the middle of raising kids in a ministry home and desperately need someone to say, "It's going to be all right." You may be in a very rough time in your marriage and struggling to find your way through. Some of you are navigating the new reality of doing ministry from an empty nest. Some couples are both in vocational ministry, and other couples will have one spouse in ministry while the other stays at home with the kids or works a secular job. The thing we all have in common is we are deeply invested in being faithful in ministry and fruitful in marriage, and we all know how challenging both can be.

Our hope is not that you'll want to emulate our marriage or ministry; our hope is that our stories will spark meaning-ful conversations for you as a couple. Feel free to skip the boring parts, jump to the chapters that sound more interest-ing, and disagree vehemently with our conclusions. At the end of each chapter are conversation starters we hope help you get started in a conversation that brings hope or at least sparks it. We encourage you to go at your own pace, pick the parts that are most meaningful along the way, and take a minute to laugh as well. If you're not ready to see the humor in your own story, we invite you to laugh at ours. It's okay, we do.

1

We're Expecting

My (Sherry's) grandma Thelma was true to the color of her red hair; she was spicy. When her church elected a new pastor, she immediately noted the pastor had a son just a bit older than her fourteen-year-old granddaughter and conspired that we should meet. I found out much later my grandma's best friend, Fleta, happened to have a granddaughter the same age, and the competition was on. Whose granddaughter would be the first to date the pastor's son? For my parents, actual dating was off-limits for a fourteen-year-old, but this didn't stop Thelma. Under the ruse of a weekend with the grandparents, I saw Geoff for the first time, dressed for Sunday church in dress slacks and a white-and-brown *Starsky and Hutch* belted sweater. I thought he was the cutest thing I had ever seen.

As luck would have it, our church youth groups helped us meet as well. We were both part of the Bible quiz teams (picture a slightly geeky form of Quiz bowl and answering obscure questions about the New Testament), and at a team retreat I actually got the nerve to talk to him. He was a worldly man of fifteen (I saw the wispy evidence of a mustache and knew I was in the presence of a man who shaved) and funny and smart and, oh, so grown-up. I was a goner. I was in love.

We dated for five years (after reaching my parents' requirement of the age of fifteen to date), and I remember sitting in his car on a rainy night when the conversation turned serious. Geoff shared how God had called him to ministry, to be a pastor, and maybe someday to plant a church. With a serious look, he asked how I felt about it, because he wanted us to be in ministry together.

With my heart racing, my mind quickly slid past the ministry part to what I thought he was hinting at. He was saying he wanted to marry me! He loved me! He repeated his question again. How did I feel about going into ministry? I remember thinking: *I've grown up in church, I love God with all my heart, and I love you. What else matters?* I must have satisfied his question, because on Christmas Day a few months later, over a romantic breakfast at an exclusive restaurant (the International House of Pancakes), I said yes, and Geoff and I became a *we*.

———

All these years later we are still on the long ride of doing ministry and marriage. Looking back on that rainy August night, sitting in my car in front of Sherry's house, I (Geoff) thought we'd covered all the bases on what marriage and ministry might be like. I asked Sherry if she wanted to be in ministry together and she said yes. I didn't know it then, but this became the first of many times I got Sherry to say yes to something she hadn't had enough time to completely think through. This led to massive problems later on, but we'll get to that later. All I knew in that car that night was I heard the best yes I could imagine. I had known since I first met this foxy fourteen-year-old that this was the girl I wanted to marry. She was cute, smart, and fall-down funny. She was always the life of the party, and I assumed once we were married the party would be 24/7.

For several years after that night I gave almost no thought to the expectations placed on a pastor's wife. I grew up in a pastor's home, my father grew up in a pastor's home, all my relatives on my dad's side grew up in pastors' homes. It was the only normal I knew. Since Sherry grew up in church, and her family was very involved in ministry, I assumed she knew what she was getting into. The traits of getting Sherry to say yes and then assuming she knew exactly what she said yes to almost ended our marriage a few years later. But we'll get to that later.

———

After saying yes to marriage and ministry, the next year was a whirlwind. I (Sherry) set about planning the perfect wedding, and my sweet dad smiled a patient smile as he handed over his wallet. Now that we have adult children, I have a better perspective of what must have been going through my parents' minds. *Does she know what she's getting into, moving so far away from her family and friends? Has she given any thought to being a youth pastor's wife and what being called to ministry really means?*

I didn't and I hadn't.

Two weeks after the wedding, we pulled into the parking lot of our new Houston home with a tiny moving van full of all the stuff in my parents' basement they hadn't yet thrown out. With the help of Geoff's parents, it took us all of thirty minutes to move into our tiny one-bedroom apartment.

We moved in on a Wednesday and it was the first night for me to experience a youth group meeting. None of the students had met me since we had gotten married in my hometown of St. Louis, and they were curious. How did Geoff and I meet? Where did we live and what was our apartment like? The question "How old are you?" made me cringe. I was two months shy of twenty and I realized I wasn't much older than most of the kids standing around me.

Our first weekend was an overwhelming experience. We also worked with the elementary kids on the weekend, so it was hard to meet many of the adults, but many of the parents in our youth group made a beeline to meet me. They were warm and friendly, but I felt as if the look behind their smiles was saying, "Wow, you are young!"

It wasn't long before I was invited to attend my first pastors' wives retreat. I packed my suitcase not knowing what to expect, but I looked forward to meeting some new friends. I was caught by surprise when our first activity, titled Being Alone, came with instructions to find an empty pup tent out of the many that had been set up for us on a hillside. We were supposed to spend the next two hours praying and being quiet. We were told not to talk to anyone else but to stay in our tent and hear what God had to say.

I'm all about prayer, and I'm a fan of getting quiet with God and listening to his voice, but I was nine hundred miles from home, without any girlfriends nearby, and feeling a little desperate. Because I am a rule follower, however, I did what I was told. I sat in my little tent. I read my Bible. I fidgeted. I ran out of things to talk to God about and came to the conclusion that I wasn't at all a spiritual giant like the women who surrounded me in their nearby tents.

But then I heard a rustling next door and I poked my head out. Coming straight at me on her hands and knees was the wife of the district superintendent (queen of the spiritual giants in my estimation), and she had chocolate in her hand.

She whispered: "You okay in here, honey? I thought you might need some snacks!"

She threw some chocolate in my tent and then crawled back to hers.

I thought for a minute I might have seen an angel.

While that retreat was a bit overwhelming and not at all what I expected, I did meet some friends. Some of the pastors' wives weren't at all like me, but some of them were. Margie, the tosser of chocolate, was a pure joy to be around. She laughed loud and often. She often forgot to wear her hearing aids, so it sounded like she was shouting most of the time. But she was an intense comfort to me. She was comfortable in her own skin, and I didn't realize it at the time, but she was encouraging me to discover my own skin and feel at home in it too.

Looking back, I realize as much as my experiences shaped me, so did my expectations. I guess I had pretty typical ones about what marriage would be, especially for someone who had focused on the wedding much more than the being married part. When it came to our life together, I expected marriage to be fun. I expected there would always be enough money. I expected marriage to be an extension of our dating life. We'd go to movies and eat pizza in front of the TV.

We'd talk endlessly about our hopes and dreams. We'd be tremendously happy. Sure, we'd have problems (small ones at worst), but we'd know how to work them out.

Probably the most dangerous of all: I expected Geoff to make me happy. But not just happy. Gloriously happy.

Had I ever told Geoff I expected all of these things? Well, really, why should I have to? Isn't that what marriage is all about? Having tons of fun and making the other person happy? That notion is so pregnant with unrealistic expectations we'll have to save it for another chapter.

Not only did I have big expectations for Geoff, but over the years I've realized I had unspoken and unintentional expectations about ministry as well. I expected being in ministry wouldn't be all that different from the way I grew up going to church. My dad was a board member and Sunday school superintendent. As a kid, I ran wild in the church halls while my parents were in choir practice, found the stash of candy in the children's church closet, and was generally a church brat. I knew the rhythm of weekend services: Sunday morning and Sunday night church, Wednesday night youth group, and Thursday morning women's ministry. But what I had never given a moment's thought to was the stuff a pastor did during the week, the actual ministry part.

The families in our church had lives that got messy. Kids ran away from home. Teenage boys slept with their girl-friends. Dads got arrested for drunk driving and ended up in jail. Moms decided they'd had enough and walked away.

Growing up in church, I would hear prayer requests and watch as my mom and dad would lend a hand with food or money and even a bed for folks who needed a place to stay. But now it was different. The families in our church came to Geoff and me with their broken, heartrending circumstances. And they wanted to know what to do next.

One Sunday afternoon, a teenage girl sat with us. As tears rolled down her cheeks, she told us her nineteen-year-old husband was having an affair and had left her and their baby girl. As she asked us what she should do, I remember thinking, *Holy cow, I don't have the first idea of what you should do.* I felt too young and too naive and too embarrassed. It began to dawn on me that by saying "I do," I had also said yes to a certain level of responsibility I had never considered.

I expected married life to be me and Geoff, not me and Geoff and the church. It felt like church seeped in everywhere: our conversations, our thoughts, our schedule, and even our bedroom. Our weeknights, weekends, and holidays were no longer our own. We had Wednesday night youth service and Friday night parties and New Year's Eve all-nighters. Holidays now turned into a source of stress. We couldn't visit my family until after Christmas because we needed to be at the church for Christmas Eve. Easter weekend took a huge amount of planning for an Easter egg hunt and an exhausting weekend of multiple services. The Fourth of July was a church picnic day. Geoff and I hadn't been married very long when I had the wistful thought, *I wonder what it's like to be normal and have a normal holiday?*

———

A normal holiday for me (Geoff), growing up in a pastor's home, was a church service or a church picnic. Family vacations were almost always trips to the denomination's annual national conference. I didn't resent church dominating everything about our family life because it was the only family life I knew. All of my friends went to our church, so church events were a chance to hang out with my friends. When we went to church conferences, we always stayed in a hotel with a swimming pool, which was heaven to a ten-year-old from Denver. My parents were always too busy at the conference to pay attention to me, so I swam, ate junk food, and did pretty much anything I wanted for five days. What's not to like about that kind of normal?

It took several years to realize that a life dominated by church activity wasn't ideal for a young wife and eventual mother. I think my first clue came at an all-night New Year's Eve party when our son was two months old. Sherry had to balance pretending to have fun, keeping an eye on eighty teenagers, and finding a place to nurse our son away from the prying eyes of adolescent boys. I thought: *Hmm, that's probably not ideal. Oh well, she'll be okay.* This was not my finest moment.

9

I (Sherry) was completely naive and expected people in church to always be nice. I was lucky to grow up in a family where the pastor was someone you prayed for and respected because he was the pastor. I'm sure my parents had disagreements with what went on in the church, but they very wisely didn't talk about it in front of me. I remember as a young child spending the night with my grandparents and hearing my grandpa pray out loud as he did every morning: *Lord, thank you for sending us our pastor. He's a great man of God, called by you. Use us to love him and his family well.*

One Sunday morning, after wrestling with fifty active (code word for pain in the butt) elementary kids in children's church, a mom marched up and stood two inches from my face. Confident she was going to tell me how much her daughter Melissa loved the Bible story that day, I gave her a big smile. But her Melissa had lost her hair bow, and mom wasn't happy and wanted me to find it. Right. That. Minute.

I was unprepared for the strong opinions and the need for people to tell us what they didn't like more often than telling us the things they did. I didn't realize the other women would share their opinions about who I sat with in church, what I wore, and how I did my hair. It hurt to find out even people we considered friends complained to others about how we did ministry.

Looking back, I wish we had sat down early on with a married couple who had more ministry experience. They could have helped with my perspective and helped me to see where our expectations were unreasonable. It would have been great to have another pastor's wife tell me it's going to be okay if there are people unhappy with the way we are leading ministry or not agreeing with our decisions or not liking my husband. I needed someone to tell me to not give in to pleasing everyone. Maybe then I wouldn't have gotten my feelings hurt so easily and felt like such a failure when I experienced the very normal things in ministry that everyone in ministry experiences.

Along the way I've been able to talk to other pastors' wives who have shared their stories of bumps and bruises and with pastors who have talked honestly about what they've learned. It's been fascinating to hear the stories that sounded so painful but actually turned into great moments of learning and healing. It made me think about my own experience as a new pastor's wife and the things I've learned along the way.

First (and this was huge for me), I've learned I have to admit I didn't break it and I can't fix it. A wise pastor friend told me awhile back that many times we see the problem only at the point after it's become desperate. We weren't there when their child first started going off the rails or when the marriage hit the first rough patch. It's usually a problem that has been months or years in the making, and all of that pain and mess isn't going to be fixed in a few conversations. How true.

It's tempting to have a quick and perfect solution to a broken relationship or family fracture, but I don't. And I shouldn't. I'm not a professional counselor, and it doesn't help anyone if I pretend I am. While they may expect expert advice, I need to focus on what I can uniquely do, which is to listen and love and pray. Early on I would take on others' problems as my own. I would feel bad when I didn't have an answer, and I would take on the burden of worry, feeling responsible for ending their pain and their disappointment when I couldn't. It wasn't helpful to them, me, or my marriage. I learned I needed to right-size my expectations for myself. I can be a wise listener and point them to Jesus. And that's about the end of what I can do.

I've also learned I need to pay attention to what I'm paying attention to, which are the voices in my head. My parents' expectations and how I was raised has a huge impact on what I tell myself today. Growing up, I was expected to get good grades, always be polite, and whenever there was a church event, I was expected to be there. This is fine and good, but it doesn't always translate into being a pastor's wife. You can't be at every event. You won't always perfectly plan that gathering or get an A in every relationship. Sometimes you are going to drop the ball or disappoint someone or not bring your best self to a speaking opportunity. So be it. The only perfect standard to achieve is the one in our heads, and it's a bunch of baloney.

Somewhere along the way I realized I was expecting myself to make it all okay for Geoff. I didn't want him to be disappointed when a family quit the church. I didn't want him to have to worry about who would teach that Sunday school class after the preschool teacher quit. I didn't want him to sweat over the finances when we lost two major tithers. I found myself going to ridiculous lengths to satisfy my own dependence on his happiness, trying to fill every hole in the church myself and talking him out of feeling sad or disappointed. After years of trying to manage my angst and what I thought was his, I realized my worry didn't help his challenges.

I've learned I need to recognize what my expectations are and say them out loud. Looking back, it was ridiculous to expect Geoff to always make me happy and that we would always have enough money. It was also unfair not to talk to him when I was caught by surprise by my expectations in ministry. It was confusing to him when he saw me getting all wound up over things that weren't a big deal to him. Being young and inexperienced set me up for not knowing what I didn't know, but it's not an excuse for not talking about what I was feeling along the way.

I've learned I don't always understand what I'm thinking or even how I feel about it, but I need to at least try to put it into words. "I'm not sure why I feel so funny about what happened today, but I need to tell you how it made me feel."

Sometimes just saying it to each other or to someone more experienced is a huge relief to our soul.

Sometimes our expectations can cause unnecessary fear because they aren't based on reality. Geoff and I recently talked with Sara and Ernest Smith, pastors of Front Range Christian Church, a fast-growing church plant in Castle Rock, Colorado. They have been in ministry together for more than fourteen years, and they shared their stories of expectations with us.

SARA AND ERNEST'S STORY

I (Sara) didn't think it would be so difficult the first year because we had dated for three and a half years prior, and I thought we knew each other pretty well. Then we got married and I didn't like him! I'm kidding. Before we got married, Ernest warned me he was going to be in ministry, which meant we would have no money and might end up living in a cardboard box. I didn't grow up in a pastor's home, so I thought Ernest surely must know what he was talking about. Although it's turned out to be not as hard or scary as I thought, I don't think I ever communicated what I was thinking to Ernest. I just remember him telling me often that we would be poor and asking, "Are you sure you want to marry me?" I always thought he was just trying to break up with me.

It definitely was difficult at first, but once we got over that bump of my worrying so much about adjusting to a life of ministry, things settled down. Each season has its own challenges, but we know how to work through those challenges together. As for ministry's impact on our marriage, I think ministry is a great thing you can do together, but you have to set up the right boundaries. If you don't, you will both find yourselves in fifty different places at once and disconnected from each other. I like doing ministry with Ernest, not apart from Ernest.

I (Ernest) thought marriage was going to be easy, consisting of having fun, waking up to your best friend, lots of sex, and raising kids together. I knew it was going to be work because I saw what happened if you don't work at it (my parents' marriage), but I thought it would be easier for us. We were Christ followers, I was going to be a pastor, and we had dated for three and a half years. I believed if anyone had this, we did. But it has been more challenging than I thought—and also more rewarding. I had an expectation that Sara and I would set an example for those who followed us: the youth, young adults, maybe even the older couples. I thought we would be an example to them as to how couples can create a healthy marriage. As for ministry, I thought we were going to be poor, poor, poor. I didn't think we would ever make more than about ten thousand dollars a year and we'd be living in a cardboard box. I hoped that wouldn't happen, but that is what I thought ministry was: you serve God, and he makes you poor. I also thought ministry was going to be very taxing on our relationship and my relationship with my students. I thought I'd be out every night of the week and answering my phone at all hours of the night and at the disposal of everyone else at the expense of my family. I thought others would consume me and very little would be left for my kids and for Sara.

I wish I'd understood earlier that I can create and control my own boundaries. Early on in ministry, I allowed the demands and emergencies of others to become my own emergencies. I didn't protect myself or my family the way I should have. I allowed the immediate problem of someone else to become my immediate problem. I now realize I'm not Jesus; my job, as the apostle John said of John the Baptist, is to point *to* the Light, not *be* the Light. I now understand that if I can't protect myself and my family, then I will allow the demands of others to control me and our family.

I also wish I'd have spent more time helping my wife know who she is and what God may want to do with her. She was amazing in being a part of the ministries I led for many years, but I wish I hadn't expected her to be a part of what I did, but rather helped her find her own calling and identity. I know God created her uniquely, but it took me a few years before I understood that maybe her calling was not to be a leader in every ministry I oversaw but rather to do and be what God called her to do and be. She is an incredible pediatric nurse and this is where she shines. She loves helping children, but that doesn't mean she has to lead our children's ministry. I need to allow her to be Sara both inside and outside the church.

Ministry has made a profound impact on our marriage. It has challenged me to be a better husband and leader, as I know others are watching us. It has helped us figure out more of who we are as individuals, who we are as a couple, and who we want to be as a family. Ministry has taught me sacrifice, not just for God, but for Sara and our kids. Ministry has helped us see that our family has a purpose and that God wants to use our family unit to impact and reach people.

WHAT DO YOU EXPECT?

If you're in the early stages of a life of ministry and marriage, it will save you years of challenges to really wrestle with the question of expectations now. Do you have expectations of what your finances will look like? How you will spend your weekends? Begin by asking yourself what thoughts are in your head that your spouse doesn't know you have. What experience do either or both of you have living in a pastor's home? What do you know and what do you think you know about the impact of ministry on marriage? Use the questions below to begin the discussion with your spouse.

TO TALK ABOUT

- What expectations did you have about your spouse when you were coming into marriage? Does your spouse know about them?

- How have your past experiences or how you grew up shaped how you feel about the ministry?

- What expectations do you put on yourself? Are they based on reality or on voices from the past?

- If you could give one piece of advice to a couple just starting in ministry, what would it be? Do you see it working in your own life?

2

Calling Card

When I (Geoff) was fifteen years old I went on a retreat with my church youth group. One evening we sat around the fireplace in the lodge where we were staying, some of the teenagers in folding chairs, others plopped in beanbags. After a couple of silly games and a few songs accompanied by an acoustic guitar, we settled in to listen to the guest speaker. I have no idea who the speaker was or what his talk was about. I'm sure it was a great message, possibly even life-changing, but my mind wandered. As I daydreamed I clearly felt God speaking to me. I didn't hear a voice or see a vision, but I strongly felt I was hearing from God. His message that evening in the Ozarks in the heart of Missouri was that I was to commit my life to vocational ministry. I was going to be a pastor.

The call to a life of ministry wasn't a tremendous stretch in my family. As I mentioned earlier, my dad, my grandfather, my uncles, and my brothers are all pastors. Most of my relatives who aren't pastors are married to pastors. There are dozens of Surratt pastors from coast to coast, and each one feels a unique call to ministry. Growing up, however, I did not want to be a pastor. While other kids wanted to be firefighters, police officers, and professional athletes, my goal was to become a lawyer. All I knew about being a lawyer came from watching reruns of *Perry Mason* (go watch an episode online if you have no idea who Perry Mason was), but it looked better than what my dad did for a living: counseling crazy people, preaching to bored people, and being voted on by angry people. (My view of church was slightly tainted by experience.) That changed, however, at a youth retreat in the Ozarks. From that evening on, I knew I would follow my family into full-time ministry.

Going forward I had a clear sense of direction and purpose in life. While my high school classmates stressed over whether they'd get into the college of their choice, I knew I would attend a Bible college after high school. Admittance wasn't a challenge since the only criteria at my college was that the registration check didn't bounce. When my dad offered me a job as a full-time youth pastor after my sophomore year, I dropped out and took the job. I was convinced this was the next step on my well-defined road to vocational ministry. Why would I waste another minute preparing for something I already had?

Everyone's story of calling is different. Some remember a definitive moment while others describe being drawn deeper and deeper into ministry over time. Regardless of how it comes, a sense of divine appointment can help one navigate the labyrinth of marriage and ministry. One of the biggest questions to ask early and often is, "Do I know that I know that God has called me to a unique life of ministry?"

In an article for *Christianity Today,* Gordon MacDonald told the story of a farmer who experienced what he believed was a supernatural call from God. As he was plowing his field, he looked up and saw clouds forming the letters *G, P,* and *C.* He knew immediately God was telling him to "Go Preach Christ." When he shared this divine vision with the deacons at his church, they invited him to preach the following Sunday. At the end of a rambling, almost incoherent sermon, one of the deacons pulled the farmer aside and said, "I think God was telling you to 'Go Plant Corn.'"

MacDonald went on to share four great signs that what you experience is truly a call from God.

1. *Call*: Is there a moment or period of time when you felt the definite tug of God on your heart? Beyond a talent for ministry or a heart for people, is there a "certainty that God has put His hand upon you and nudged you toward a particular people, theme, or function"?

2. *Confirmation*: Do other people affirm that they see a call of God on your life? When God sets someone aside for a special mission, he almost always confirms his call to others as well. We see this clearly in the commissioning of Paul and Barnabas in Acts 13.

3. *Giftedness*: God doesn't call us into anything we're not gifted to do. God would never call me to be the worship pastor at a church; my singing is so bad it makes children cry. Being gifted doesn't necessarily mean you are great at something, but it does mean you have the ingredients to become great.

4. *Results*: Are people influenced by your ministry? Are they drawn to Christ? Measuring the results of ministry is difficult, but wherever God gives a call there will be visible impact.[1]

While my sense of calling is not always strong, in times of doubt it is comforting to go back to that youth retreat forty years ago when I first felt God moving my heart toward a life of full-time service in the kingdom and to remember the confirmation, giftedness, and results I've experienced along the way. Whenever I lose my way, I remember that ministry is not just something I chose; it is something for which God chose me. The assignment changes, but the calling stays the same.

It is easy, however, to confuse calling with bad burritos. When I was in high school, I avoided hard classes because I reasoned things like trigonometry and foreign languages wouldn't be needed in the life of a pastor. The reality is I was being lazy and avoiding rigorous study habits that would have served me well along the way.

While I'm thankful for my early experiences as a youth pastor, dropping out of college was not a wise decision. At nineteen years of age I was not equipped for the ministry challenges that came my way. Another two to four years of education would have been incredibly beneficial. As I look back I realize I have often used the "calling card" as an excuse to do what I wanted to do. Calling is not a substitute for wisdom.

There is nowhere this lack of wisdom has wreaked more havoc than in my relationship with my wife. Early in our marriage I played the calling card often. I felt Sherry should have known what she was getting into, because I'd been very clear that God had called me to ministry, specifically as a youth pastor working for my dad in Houston. Low pay, all-night parties for teenagers, and summer camps were all part of the calling package.

For Sherry, moving nine hundred miles away from home, finishing school, and starting a family were overwhelming, and rather than deal with an understanding husband, she had to deal with an immature youth pastor armed with a calling card. After ten years as a youth pastor, I pulled out the calling card when I felt it was time to be a lead pastor at a tiny church in a tiny Texas town. And a few years later the calling card came out again when given the opportunity to move to South Carolina and work with my brother at a church plant in Charleston. While calling played a part in each of these decisions, and God used each move to grow us, using calling as a manipulative lever was always damaging.

As I matured I realized God's call on my life is less about where I work and what I do and more about how I share the gospel by loving people. I have a friend who talks about big-C calling and little-c calling. Throughout the Bible there are examples of both. When God told Noah to build a boat, that was a big-C calling. God was very specific about when, where, and how Noah was to fulfill what he was being asked to do. Noah could obey or not obey, but there was no doubt about his specific assignment.

But when Jesus called his disciples, it was more of a little-c calling. "Jesus called out to them, 'Come, follow me, and I will show you how to fish for people!'" (Matt. 4:19). He didn't give them a job description or even a title. He simply called them to follow him. His charge at the end of his ministry was equally vague: "Go and make disciples." It seems that as long as they were making disciples, they were being faithful to their call.

I'm learning that God's call is most often lived out in how I treat others—beginning at home. Colossians 3 has a clear picture of what God's calling looks like in relationships:

> Since God chose you to be the holy people he loves, you must clothe yourselves with tenderhearted mercy, kindness, humility, gentleness, and patience. Make allowance for each other's faults, and forgive anyone who offends you. Remember, the Lord forgave you, so you must forgive others. Above all, clothe yourselves with love, which binds us all together in perfect harmony. And let the peace that comes from Christ rule in your hearts. For as members of one body you are called to live in peace. And always be thankful. (vv. 12–15)

I love to think about calling in terms of ministry goals and opportunities, but if I'm not displaying "tenderhearted mercy, kindness, humility, gentleness, and patience" to my family, it doesn't matter what kind of ministry I am leading. I am missing my calling. I often must step back from the intoxicating and overwhelming tasks of ministry and ask if I am truly fulfilling God's plan for my life. Am I being a loving husband? Am I present for my children? Does my family see the gospel reflected in the way I live out my faith at home? The keys for me are to be sure of my calling and not to use that calling as a shortcut in relationships.

As challenging as calling is for me, it is even more complicated for Sherry. When we married, she became something called a pastor's wife. Is that a role she should be called to? Is there a job description? What if she wants to be my wife, but God has wired her up to minister outside of the church?

IS "PASTOR'S SPOUSE" A CALLING?

I (Sherry) struggled with this throughout the first half of our marriage. What's the role of a pastor's wife? What is she supposed to do and know and be? It was a mystery to me since I hadn't grown up in a pastor's home. I had grown up in a conservative church where the pastor's wife wore only dresses past the knee and was never seen without panty hose or beehive hair. She led the women's ministry and helped organize quilt making for the missionary wives. Panty hose made me sweat, and my home economics sewing project earned a D.

While Geoff was in Bible college and I was in a Christian liberal arts college in the same town, I remember going on a double date with Geoff's roommate and his girlfriend who had grown up in a pastor's home. As she told me about her dad's church, I watched as she deftly made a salad for our picnic lunch in the park. Instead of attacking the head of lettuce with a knife (the only method I knew), she smacked it smartly on the picnic table, neatly dislodging the core. She then whipped up a fancy green-leaf affair that would have made Martha Stewart proud.

She quipped, "You'll need to know this trick because, as a pastor's wife, you'll be making lots of salads for all the church dinners."

As I mentioned before, the only thing I knew how to whip up was mac and cheese—that is, the fake kind in the blue box.

My insecurities led me down a bad trail as we began our ministry life. Geoff was not only the youth pastor but also the children's pastor, and I was right by his side. Sunday mornings I taught in children's ministry, Sunday nights I helped with the middle school group, and Wednesday nights I helped lead worship in the student ministry. When Geoff transitioned into a lead pastor role of a church plant, I felt the pressure to fill every hole. We needed to start a children's ministry and the women wanted a women's ministry and we needed a worship leader for Sunday mornings. It was the makings of a hair-on-fire disaster.

It would have been a tremendous gift if I'd had the sense to lean toward another pastor's wife who could have sat me down and given me permission to slow down and assess my situation. I had young children to raise. I was a teacher who truly felt God's calling to teach in public school. I had a husband who was working long hours and needed a wife who wasn't too exhausted to pay attention to him.

If you're a young pastor's wife reading this right now, here are a couple of things I know about you. You are probably one of the sharpest and most talented women in the church. You have a deep passion for serving God and others, and I bet you have church experience either as a volunteer or a staff member. These are great things. But don't let this take you down a self-destructive path. You have to discover your own calling and follow God's direction for your journey.

Here are a few things I wish I would have let sink in earlier. Just because there's a ministry hole doesn't mean you're the plug. Take the time to sit with God and ask him who he designed you to be. Then be that. If you are a stay-at-home wife or mom who focuses solely on being a great support for her husband, then be the best one you can be and don't feel guilty about it. If there's an area of the church you are passionate about, and it fits into your life and gift set, go for it. If God has equipped you to use your talents outside the church and this is where your passion lies, be the best teacher or CEO or *whatever* you can be.

Sure, there are times when you may need to step in and help fill a hole because it needs to be done (who really feels called to the ministry of changing diapers?), but don't be trapped by guilt-ridden shoulds. You can be sure of this: God called you to be the best wife and mom your husband and kids could ever need or want. Whatever else God calls you to do or be is icing on the ministry cake.

My (Geoff's) mom modeled this concept. She was a great role model for other pastors' wives because she never fell into the trap of trying to be anything other than what God created her to be. She didn't work outside the home, because she felt called to stay at home with her four children. She volunteered in areas of ministry at church where she felt gifted to serve, and she didn't serve where she didn't want to.

Mom loved to teach teen Sunday school classes, and she was very good at it. She did not, however, like to lead women's Bible studies. In fact, she didn't even like attending women's Bible studies, so she seldom did. This did not sit well with some ladies in the church, and they tried to pressure her into areas where she didn't want to serve. But Mom didn't give in to pressure. She had a strong sense of who she was and who God created her to be and she was very comfortable in her role.

My dad supported my mom by informing the elders at churches where he pastored that they had hired him, not his wife and family. Mom's advice to young pastors' wives was always to discover who God created them to be and not let anyone else decide their role in ministry.

FIVE *C*'S OF CALLING

As we wrap up the discussion on the role of calling in your marriage, we want to give you five *C*'s we find helpful in this area.

1. *Communicate*: One of the most important conversations you can have as a couple is around the area of calling. Spend some time discussing your understanding of what calling looks like in the life of ministry. Share your story of calling. Can you point to a specific time and place, or is it more of a general sense of purpose? If you don't feel a specific calling to ministry or to be married to someone in ministry, discuss what that means. Connect with other ministry couples and ask about their sense of calling.

   It is also important to discuss the feelings that go with this sense of calling. Does your spouse ever feel manipulated by your use of the calling card? Did your spouse know what was involved when signing up for when they married someone significantly involved in ministry? Many spouses of pastors say they secretly wish their husband or wife would find another line of work. Is this true in your marriage? These are very difficult questions to ask but incredibly important in the process of following God in the context of a healthy marriage.

2. *Clarify*: What has God specifically called you to? As we shared earlier, when Geoff was a sophomore in high school, he believed God specifically called him to be a pastor, but he decided to drop out of college and become a youth pastor at nineteen. How specific

is your calling? Could you live out the calling on your life in a variety of arenas or has God given you a big-C, Noah-type calling?

3. *Confirm*: If God is calling you to a new ministry, a new church, or a new town, he will confirm that call in your spouse. As the apostle Paul said in 1 Corinthians 14:33, God is not the author of disorder but of peace. If you feel called but your spouse does not, it's not time to make a move. It might be the wrong move or the wrong time.

A few years ago I (Geoff) was convinced the next ministry move in our lives was to move to Dallas and work for a nonprofit organization. We discussed the move for several weeks, weighing the pros and cons. When it came time to make the final decision, Sherry said she didn't have a peace about the move. I was incredibly frustrated and was sure she was wrong, but I knew if she wasn't in agreement, it either wasn't the right time or the right move. Looking back, now we know it was the wrong time and the wrong move. We were saved from a wrong step because Sherry heard clearly from God when I was listening to my gut. You have to have faith that God will speak to both of you about your next move.

God will also confirm a definite call through trusted Christian mentors. God seldom works in a vacuum. If he is working in your heart, he will be working in the hearts of others as well. Every feeling of calling needs to be run through the filter of wise men and women willing to speak truth into your life. If you don't find confirmation in people who know you well and who you trust completely, it's likely not the right time or the right move.

4. *Create a "calling description"*: As you process calling in each of your lives, consider writing a calling description. What do each of you feel specifically called to? What does this calling entail and not entail? One of the realities of ministry is that others will set clear expectations for you if you fail to set them yourself. And the healthiest place to set expectations is in the context of family.

5. *Commit*: As we look back on three decades of ministry, we have served in almost every existing ministry capacity. We've led children's ministry and youth ministry. We've been lead pastors, executive pastors, and associate pastors. We've worked full-time secular jobs while holding significant ministry positions, and we've worked for nonprofits while volunteering in a local church. During all the changes we've experienced, one thing has remained, namely, our call to faithfully shepherd God's people. Within that calling there's a lot of leeway around location, role, and compensation.

What does not change is the commitment to love
God with all our heart, mind, soul, and strength
and to love our neighbors as ourselves.

Whatever else you do in life, be faithful to your calling.

TO TALK ABOUT

- Have you ever expressed to your spouse what you feel God has called you to be and do? See if you can express it to your spouse in just a few sentences.

- Do you feel like you get to operate fully in that calling? If not, what do you think holds you back?

- How are you each doing in supporting each other's calling? Share your appreciation and any thoughts on how your spouse might support you even further.

- Are there any feelings of resentment around how calling has played out in your marriage? Take a few minutes to talk it over and spend some time praying together.

3

Together Separate

We've always wondered what life is like for ministry couples who always seem to be pursuing the same dream. They are both focused on the same church, the same ministry, and the same goals. Some couples both work for the same church, and sometimes one works at the church while the other one stays home, but they see themselves as walking the same path. If that describes you, we envy the clarity that must bring. (You will likely want to skip this chapter.) That has seldom been our story. While we've always supported each other's dreams, those dreams have often been in different arenas.

I (Sherry) always knew I would be a schoolteacher. I was one of those weird kids who loved every minute of school, and in the third grade I assigned myself homework, pretending I was my own teacher (I probably should never admit that). To this day I find something enticing about the smell of fresh paper and crayons. Though it's been many years since I have been a classroom teacher, I still find myself in Target every fall with the sole purpose of running my hands over the pens and markers and three-ring binders. I know, it's a little creepy.

I've known since I was a high-school sophomore I would be a teacher, so for the first years of our marriage I focused on finishing my teaching degree and looked forward to my own classroom. Sometimes during those early years, as I daily commuted fifty miles back and forth to college, there were moments when I wondered what I was doing. Our lives we're already chaotic with all of the pressure of leading the children's and student ministries in a growing church. Did I really need to pursue a teaching degree? I had lots of opportunities to work with kids already. I knew, however, just as Geoff had been called to full-time ministry, I was called to be a public-school teacher. Being in front of a roomful of kids, helping them make sense of fractions and paragraphs, thrilled me, and I knew I was wired to be a teacher. So I did my student teaching, got my degree, and began looking for a full-time teaching job. And then we had a surprise.

I decided to surprise Geoff at work with the good news: "Hey, sweetheart, you're going to be a dad."

There was a moment of stunned silence.

"You mean a baby? You're going to have a baby?" He was smiling, but his face had a funny look. A look that said, "I need air."

I took a deep breath. "That's usually the way it works. And it's 'we.' *We* are going to have a baby." I was so excited I could hardly stand it. I was hoping Geoff was excited too. We had talked about it, but I felt like I'd just delivered an unexpected baby bomb. I could guess what was going through his mind. How will this fit in our life? How much does a baby cost? Do we know how to be parents?

A MAN'S PERSPECTIVE

When Sherry walked into my office that morning, she looked like she'd just won the lottery. To her the news that she—I mean we—were going to have a baby was the best thing ever for her. I knew that it was a possibility some day in the distant future, but I had never considered the implications of having a baby *now*.

All those implications hit me like a cold shower: Sherry was barely out of college, and I was still figuring out how to be a youth pastor. Sherry drove our only car, which ran sporadically, and I rode a motorcycle. How was I going to strap a car seat to a motorcycle? I think we had $23.54 in our checking account, which was more than we had in savings. I was smart enough to know this was not the moment to bring up these fairly significant obstacles in our path to parenthood. I put on my best fake excited look and said something like: "A baby! I couldn't be more excited! Oh goodie!" I knew she didn't buy it.

Our firstborn, Mike, joined the Surratt family with long, skinny arms and the most gorgeous blue eyes I had ever seen. He had big feet that made the nurses say, "Wow, you're going to be spending a lot of money on shoes." And just like that, we went from Sherry and me to Sherry and me and Mike.

We were crazy about our new son, but the challenges I worried about before Mike was born were all real, and there were many times we didn't have a clue as to how we were going to make ends meet. Sherry stayed home with Mike for the first year, which was awesome for them and a killer on our already meager finances. The interesting thing, however, is that somehow we made it. It seems like when you are pursuing God's best in ministry, in marriage, and in parenting, things have a way of working out. We were poor and clueless and right in the middle of God's will for our lives.

Having Mike, however, didn't change Sherry's commitment to education. He was almost two when she started teaching and life really got crazy.

A WOMAN'S PERSPECTIVE

I (Sherry) remember working during the day, rushing home, cooking dinner with Mike on my hip, and then many nights scooping him up as we joined Geoff for youth group or something else at church. After our daughter, Brittainy, was born, Geoff had an opportunity to plant a church thirty minutes from where we lived (we'll talk about this wild ride in a later chapter), so now we added a hefty commute to our church life. I bet many of you can relate to the fact that sometimes there just aren't words big enough to describe how crazy life can get.

I've often asked myself questions such as "Am I doing the right thing by continuing to pursue my passions of teaching and leadership?" "Am I spread in too many directions to be a good support for Geoff?" You must be honest with yourself and God when you answer these questions. I also know that what's right for me may not be right for anyone else. You must decide, based on who you are and what God has called you to be. Your church can't answer these questions for you; this is where together as husband and wife you get to wrestle it to the ground.

I'm still learning who I am, what I'm good at, and what I'm not. I have been a teacher and a family ministry pastor, worked for nonprofits, and served as a CEO. I love to work. In the church and in other endeavors, I love to use my gifts of strategic thinking and planning to make things better. I've learned to get comfortable and be confident in my own decision making when it comes to being a mom, a wife, and an employee. I've had times when I've had to say no to a church opportunity because it wasn't possible to juggle with my family and outside job. Sometimes I've had to say no to work because I needed to be home or at church. While I don't believe in perfect balance (I don't think Jesus did either. See chapter 5.), I do believe in a healthy ebb and flow that coincides with what my family and church need in different seasons. I wish I could say I've handled it well every day. But there are a couple of things I've learned along the way.

Paying Attention to Myself

I've learned I need to pay attention to what's going on inside me. I remember riding in the passenger seat on our way to Church on the Lake (our church plant) for Wednesday service. It had been a long day at school and I felt if I had to smile or talk to one more person my head might explode. *Please, Lord, don't let the piano player corner me before I even get a cup of coffee, and if I get stuck working in the nursery again, I'm going to give myself a nosebleed.* These were my holy thoughts as our car sped down the freeway.

I remember looking over at Geoff, who was deep in thought about what he was going to talk about that night. I thought: *This just isn't fair. I'm at school all day, doing my job, and now I have to spend my evenings helping him do his.* My thoughts and emotions were in a big twist. As we got out of the car I barked at Geoff, at my kids, and probably anyone else who cornered me inside.

What was really going on was crabby exhaustion. I loved our church and the people, and I was incredibly proud of Geoff for everything he was accomplishing. But I was tired. And hungry. I had fed the kids but didn't take time to eat properly myself and had grabbed a huge handful of M&M's as I headed out the door. Big food fail.

Days like this are going to happen to everyone. Sometimes they indicate you need to rearrange your life, but at other times it's simply a matter of taking care of yourself along the way and being adult enough to admit when you haven't. Don't let the fact that you need a hamburger and a nap drive you to conclude your life isn't working.

When working in separate careers, it can become a wall between the two of you if you let it. I've learned I need to invite Geoff into my work. Not just talk to him about what I did that day, but invite him to join me in what's going on. From talking to other couples in ministry who have separate careers, I've come to realize this is a big deal. Geoff has incredible skills that I don't, and it helps me when I lean into what he's good at. I remember feeling anxious about a talk I had to give at a conference, and when Geoff asked me about it, I shut him off with a clipped, "It's fine!" I didn't realize this hurt us both. It made him feel like I didn't value his opinion and didn't need his help, and it left me continuing to stew in my anxiety. I felt like he was already having to speak so much, he would hate it if I asked for help. But he welcomed being invited in, and it made him feel needed and loved. And my talk became *much* better with his help.

On the flip side, I appreciate it when Geoff asks for my thoughts about ministry as well as asking for my help in filling a ministry need. We talk about sermon ideas, staffing possibilities, and ministry strategy together. When he asks, I try to bring an objective outside perspective and offer it with open hands. If he doesn't like an idea I offer, I need to be okay with that.

For Geoff, it's important to not just talk about what I do but to invite him into the how and what. It has made a difference when I've invited him to meet the teams I work with. It makes him feel like a part of me and what I'm doing even though he can't do it every day. It takes the *me* in my passion and turns it into a *we,* which makes it even more fun.

In ministry, there's always something more that needs to be done, and there are lots of opportunities for the other spouse to join in. But when one spouse has a job that isn't ministry-related, it takes more intentionality. Even if you can't help your spouse with what they do day to day, you can still be their champion. Look for where you see their talent at work and call it out. Our friend Phil Vaughan opens every newcomers gathering by talking about his wife and her nursing job and how incredibly good she is at it. He often tells others that it's her ministry outside the walls of the church and it makes him incredibly proud.

Paying Attention to Each Other

Along the way we've also learned it's important to support each other in pursuing our passion. When I got the call to join Mothers of Preschoolers (MOPS International) as their CEO, my immediate thought was, *No way, that's too big of a job for me.* I had all kinds of negative thoughts. *Are they nuts? They don't know I don't have the experience to do that or they wouldn't have asked me.* When I shared my thoughts with Geoff, he said, "Of course you can do this. You've got this!" My taking this job meant we would have to move from California to Denver, and for Geoff, it would mean leaving his position at Saddleback Church and having to figure out what he would do next. He didn't hesitate. He was my biggest champion then and he still is.

Every year at MOPS, Geoff came to our annual leadership conference. Picture three thousand young moms excited to be away from their kids, emotions running high with the fun of a girlfriend weekend—and Geoff. The poor guy couldn't find a bathroom because that many women had taken over every restroom in the place. As I waited backstage on the first night to speak, one of the security guys told me they had been called to check out a strange man who was hanging out at the back of the auditorium. It was Geoff.

He had no thoughts of being a mom creeper. He wanted to be there. To be available. For me. I remember coming onstage at my first conference and seeing him in the front row, looking straight into my eyes with a look that said, "You can do this!"

———

I (Geoff) am an introvert, so attending any conference with three thousand people is a stretch for me. But attending a conference of three thousand women and only one man—me—was beyond uncomfortable. The last night of the annual conference is called MomProm, which is exactly what it sounds like: a dance for all the young moms.

I tried to be a supportive husband and went with Sherry to the first MomProm. When we walked in, there were several thousand women dancing to "Macarena." I told Sherry, "I love you, but I gotta get out of here," and I found a place where I could eat a big, juicy burger and watch college football.

In many ways, though, MOPS was a great experience. Up until then I had always been onstage, people asked for my advice, and conference leaders invited me to speak. When I was with Sherry at MOPS, I was simply her husband. Ladies often asked me to take their picture with Sherry or they'd ask me for a pen so Sherry could sign their copy of her book. It wasn't just humbling (though it was humbling), it was amazing! Sherry was able to use her gifts, completely out of any shadow I might cast, to minister to women all over the world.

One of the coolest things we did while she was at MOPS was attend the annual MOPS convention in Australia. (I was the lone man at the conference—again.) Women half a world away were becoming better *mums* and Christ followers through a ministry Sherry was leading. I am so glad Sherry followed God's call on her life to become the unique leader he created her to be.

WE MAKE A GREAT TEAM

I (Sherry) have been a youth camp counselor for more summers than I can count. Year after year I spent a sweaty week with students playing wallyball and spraying shaving cream in each other's pillows. I loved it because Geoff was a phenomenal youth pastor and I loved being a part of how God used him. He dreamed up incredible games that drew kids in; he challenged them to lift their eyes up just a bit and see what God was doing all around them. When he spoke, I heard God's words coming out of his mouth. I wouldn't have missed it for the world.

Today, as Geoff is helping lead a church plant team get off the ground, he still amazes me. I see him encouraging and mentoring, sharing his strategic thinking and wisdom, and it makes me proud to be his wife. Just last week we had a block party to celebrate the church's one-year anniversary, and as I watched Geoff helping in every area from setup to preaching and everything in between, I again realized that while our gifts are different and we often minister in separate arenas, we make a great team.

UP IN EACH OTHER'S BUSINESS

What if you both work at the same church in different departments? Geoff and I have done this as well. At Seacoast Church in Mt. Pleasant, South Carolina, Geoff worked as the family ministry pastor and then moved into the executive pastor role. Seacoast then hired me as the children's ministry pastor, which meant I was Geoff's replacement and he was now my boss. If that makes you shudder, I don't blame you. Imagine when salary review time rolled around and the uncomfortable place it put him in. Even worse, imagine performance review time.

Me: What do you mean you think that event could have been better and I'm over budget?

Him: (Uncomfortable silence. And cue a tense dinner that evening.)

Actually Geoff and I were able to make it work, although we don't recommend it for everyone. We consciously tried not to tromp on each other's areas or give advice where it wasn't wanted. We set firm times during which we didn't talk about the church. I had to try hard not to let my feelings get hurt when Geoff didn't tell me everything that happened or when he made executive decisions about the areas I led. There were lots of moments when I had to have a talk with myself and allow Geoff to be who he was: my boss at work and my husband and best friend at home. We tried to take advantage of the times we did get to work together and to have fun doing it, which helped us both learn something incredibly powerful: we are better *together* when we are our *individual* best.

GREG AND SUSAN'S STORY

We first met Greg and Susan Ligon through Leadership Network, a company committed to helping churches in collaborative innovation. Greg and Susan, both authors and accomplished in the fields of publishing and leading church innovation, have two nearly grown boys. They still have managed to carve out a life where they both pursue individual careers while managing a business built around a shared passion. When I visited their house and saw they both work from home in the same space, with their desks just a few feet apart, I knew this was a couple that knew how to work well in ministry both separately and together. We asked them to tell us their story and what they've learned.

～

Susan and I (Greg) met in 1989 when she was singing in my administrative assistant's son's wedding. I'm actually surprised she talked to me. I was wearing a suit and bow tie, and I learned later she thought bow ties were goofy. Shortly after we met, I moved to Dallas to start a new student ministry at Southern Methodist University (SMU) and to be close to Susan, who had begun a career in marketing and public relations at Word Publishing. After several near misses, I convinced her to lower her standards and say yes and then "I do" on May 1, 1993. Early in our marriage, Susan shared ministry with me at SMU while she served great authors like Chuck Swindoll and Max Lucado.

A little over three years later, we were blessed with our first son, Daniel, and twenty-three months later we welcomed Andrew into our family. Today, Daniel is twenty and a sophomore at Baylor University, and Andrew is eighteen and completing his senior year of high school and exploring his college options for the fall. Susan had planned to be a stay-at-home mom, caring for our children, but when Daniel wasn't quite a year old, we both began new career endeavors. Susan began working on Max Lucado's publishing and branding team, and I joined the leadership team at Leadership Network. Life was busy, but we sensed a common passion to help authors and organizations "see what could be."

We decided to form the Ligon Group, an independent

company that helped these entities "form the pathway to see what could be." It has been nineteen years since we began our separate-yet-together journey, and it's been a grand adventure.

While our passions and gifts definitely overlap, our work styles are very different, and we respect that in each other. I like to have a designated space I can make my own. Susan can work *anywhere* and does—from the office to the library to the kitchen table. Variety creates energy for her and frustration for me. Fortunately, we have space where we can both create our ideal environments. And we have learned (and are still learning) how to flex as projects and schedules demand.

We both love the flexibility that working from home affords, but it's not perfect. It's tempting to be all up in each other's business, but we respect each other's gifting. We don't give each other unwanted advice, but we offer input and perspective when it's solicited. One of the issues of working in the same company—a company you both created—is there are times you have to work together when, honestly, you just don't feel like it. Sometimes you have to act your way into a new way of feeling so you can make it to the finish line.

About a dozen years ago, we did a major brand analysis for a leading author. Our kids were young and demanding, and we were tired. We would put the boys to bed and then dig in and get as much done as we could before collapsing into bed and then rising again to do it the next day and the next. We survived this four-month project only with the support of grandparents who helped with the boys, lots of black coffee, and the grace of God. Were we always pleasant with each other? No, but again and again we came back to the belief that we had something to contribute that would accelerate and maximize the ministry.

The biggest challenges are time, focus, and prioritization. Susan's work is pretty much full-time. My work at Leadership Network is definitely full-time. But God continues to provide opportunities for us to serve other authors, ministries, and even corporations to see what can be and to develop pathways to get there. So our most difficult challenge is learning when to say no (an uncomfortable word in our vocabulary).

Some of our biggest surprises have been seeing how God brought us together and how our gifts serve to complete each other in so many ways, including the work he has called us to do. We are fortunate that we love many of the same things, both inside and outside our work. So when we aren't working, we are together: running errands, hanging out with friends, providing leadership for the high school baseball booster club. You name it, we do it together.

~

It has surprised me (Susan) how much fun it still is after twenty-three years of marriage. I still get a charge when something really comes together well and it's clear we can do things together we could never do apart.

We love to spend time with other young couples who are in ministry together, and here's what we tell them:

- Give each other the best of yourselves, including your humility and forgiveness.
- Seek to listen first.
- Make time for connection outside of ministry.
- Be intentionally intergenerational.
- Look for ways to share life with other couples that are ahead of you on the marriage-family cycle who can show you the way on the things you don't have a clue about.
- Find other couples in the same stage of life so you have someone to share war stories with.
- Look for ways to share life with those behind you on the marriage road, hopefully helping them to avoid some of the dumb taxes you've paid along the way.

We love Greg and Susan's story of their separate areas of expertise utilized in a common passion. Maybe as you've read this chapter it's sparked thoughts of things you appreciate about your spouse that you've never told them. Or maybe it's stirred thoughts of frustration or resentment that you've never talked about. Now is a great time. Use these questions to guide your conversation.

TO TALK ABOUT

- If you work in separate vocations, how do you affirm the *we* in your marriage and ministry?

- Is there tension about the ways you serve each other's vocations (or don't serve) that you haven't talked about? What would you like to say to each other right now?

- Are there ways you'd like to be involved in the other's work that you are not?

- If you work together at your church, do you have open communication about how it affects your relationship? Is there anything you'd like to tell your spouse that you haven't?

4

Together Alone

The words *"Sweetheart, what would you think about our taking over a church plant in Huffman?"* rocked my world. Geoff and I had been at The Tab (short for Assembly of God Tabernacle in Houston) for ten years. Geoff was a family ministry pastor, and I was a testing coordinator at my school, set to move into an assistant principal role. Our kids were doing great, and we had lots of friends in the church. I liked life the way it was. His question left me thinking, *Why would we want to do that?*

I could tell God was up to something in Geoff's heart by the way he asked the question. Huffman is a rural town on the far side of Lake Houston, and it was farther away in culture than it was in distance. A friend later described the difference between Huffman and Houston: "Well, you see, it's like this. The women in Houston and Huffman are mostly the same, but the women in Houston are more likely to have all their teeth."

I went with Geoff the Sunday morning he was asked to "try out." It was a combination of *American Idol* and *Survivor*, during which they listened to a pastor's best sermon and then decided if they'd vote him off the island. That night they brought us back to get to know us better. We sat in the dingy fellowship hall—a double-wide trailer that served as their children's church—as the eleven church members bombarded us with questions. I wondered what in the world we were getting ourselves into. There was no children's program, no staff, and a very small church building that needed lots of repairs. I looked at Geoff and was shocked to see he seemed to be enjoying the process.

They called the next day with an invitation for Geoff to become the pastor of Church on the Lake. The vote had been nine for, one against, and one abstention: a landslide. Geoff was excited to go; he felt God was calling him to lead the people of Huffman and become lead pastor of this struggling church plant. I was willing to go only because Geoff was excited.

Our first Sunday was hard. All eleven people who voted were there, plus a few other curious folks. I looked around and wondered what to help with first. The greeter at the door was a friendly man who welcomed everyone with a big hug and a loud hello. We soon discovered that was the only English word he knew. He was also the drummer in the worship band, and his rhythm was only slightly better than his English.

The pianist also was rhythm-challenged, so the musical portion of the service was rough. After we stumbled through a few songs, one of the members made a couple of announcements and then introduced Geoff. I listened to my husband with pride as he talked about how much God loved this church and the people in it and how God wanted to transform Huffman.

There was so much to do and we jumped in. During the next few months we started a children's ministry, built a worship team, started renovations on the church building, and began to meet the neighbors. We organized a few workdays, which included painting, cleaning out the worship auditorium, and clearing the sidewalk of the goose droppings left by the feathered friends who called the lake "home." As we stacked the stained 1970s hymnals at the back of the room, a woman who had helped start the church made a beeline for Geoff.

"What are you going to do with the hymnals?" she asked.

"We're going to throw them in the Dumpster," he answered.

She couldn't have looked any more stunned if Geoff had slapped her with a kitten. Things were off to a rough start.

A few weeks later another matriarch of the church stopped Geoff at the end of a Sunday service.

"Did you know there was one abstention when you were voted on?" she asked.

"I heard something like that," Geoff replied, not sure where this conversation was going.

"I was the one who abstained," she explained. "I didn't feel like I knew you well enough to vote. But now that I do, my husband and I will be leaving the church."

With that we lost our women's ministry director, our Spanish-speaking greeter, and our drummer. Quickly we had grown the church from eleven to nine.

I was unprepared for the unfiltered criticism that came our way from that day on. From my vantage point it felt as if we were doing our best, but our best just wasn't working. Eventually the church began to grow, but those first few months were brutal.

WHAT WAS HE THINKING?

For me (Geoff), Church on the Lake was the chance of a lifetime. A few years before, while I was a youth pastor working for my dad, I attended a church growth conference at Willow Creek Community Church in the western suburbs of Chicago. It was unlike any church I'd ever seen. They used theatrical lighting, secular music, and dramatic sketches to present the gospel in a modern and relevant way. They intentionally targeted seekers rather than the "already convinced." I walked away from that conference believing the Willow Creek model was exactly what I was wired to do. All I needed was an opportunity. Church on the Lake was that opportunity. We were going to create a modern church with modern music and modern sermons in rural Texas. What could possibly go wrong?

One Sunday, not long after becoming pastor, I unleashed Willow Creek on Huffman. A friend sang a cover of the Eagles' "Life in the Fast Lane." Another friend did a one-man pantomime called "The Plate Spinner." And I preached a word-for-word version of a Bill Hybels sermon. At the end, the handful of people in the congregation looked stunned and confused. The sweet little ladies of the congregation asked their husbands what had happened to their little church. It wasn't the stunning success I had envisioned.

The next two and a half years were a struggle as I gradually realized that small-town Texas had almost nothing in common with suburban Chicago. I wasn't pastoring doctors, lawyers, and bankers; these were salt-of-the-earth people who loved God but struggled with life.

One Sunday after church, one of the matriarchs of the church asked to speak to me privately in my office. When we sat down, she began to cry and said she was in big trouble. I wondered if there was a problem with one of her grandkids or maybe a financial challenge.

"Pastor Geoff," she explained, "I was arrested for transporting marijuana into a Texas state prison."

I asked her to repeat that, because it was difficult to believe sweet little Sister D—had been a drug mule. She confirmed she was out on bail and facing trial for a felony. If you've watched *The Andy Griffith Show*, imagine Aunt Bee facing five to ten in the big house. Nothing in Bible college prepares you for days like this.

I flashed back to sitting at the church growth conference several years before, dreaming of excellent music, thought-provoking drama, and relevant messages. It never occurred to me then that God would call me to pastor tax-evading Sunday school teachers, illiterate wrecker drivers, and recently incarcerated grandmothers. In the midst of my disillusionment with the reality of ministry, I completely lost track of the most important person in my life. While I struggled to bring Willow Creek to Huffman, I passively watched my marriage slowly unravel.

THE BEGINNING OF THE END

Looking back, I (Sherry) can see the things we accomplished and also where we made mistakes. Geoff was doing all the preaching, leading, and speaking. He was even mowing the church lawn. I was leading worship, teaching kids' church, leading women's ministry, plus working full-time at a teaching job.

We were both beyond exhaustion, but even worse, we weren't paying attention to what was going on in each other's hearts. Geoff was discouraged. While the church had grown to over a hundred, it wasn't growing as fast as he expected. Money was tight, he still didn't have any paid staff, and with all the changes, the original core (those who were left of the original eleven) were grumbling.

Geoff's discouragement made me uncomfortable, but I had my own issues. I was caught up in resentment. I loved my teaching job, but piled on with all the things I was leading at the church, I felt completely overwhelmed. I worried that our kids were missing out by being in such a small church that barely had a children's ministry. I watched Geoff work so hard but felt resentful that no one was stepping up to help. I felt every ebb and flow of growth intensely and became dependent on it. When our attendance was up, life was good. When our attendance was down, I wanted to give up. I didn't realize it at the time, but I was on codependence overload, with God barely in sight.

What was going on was hard to talk about. I remember standing on the front porch of the church with Geoff on a Sunday morning, watching the few cars pull in, when Geoff said, "I saw the guitar was gone from backstage this morning. I think the guitar player quit the church. Once again we have no worship band." I ached for him. I heard the pain, but I felt powerless to help. I was just too tired.

After almost two and a half years, Geoff decided to leave. The disappointment of ministry, the pain of people walking away, and the strain on the family became too much. He took a job teaching high school and then a job teaching computer software. He walked away from vocational ministry exhausted and disillusioned. It felt as if ministry were over, but maybe our marriage would get better.

And it did. Until it got worse.

THE END

After a year of teaching, Geoff got a call from his brother Greg to help him at Seacoast Church in Charleston, South Carolina. The church was growing quickly and they needed help. To Geoff this seemed like a return from exile.

I struggled with this in my heart. I had been promoted to assistant principal and just found out I was going to be promoted to principal. This is what I had worked hard for, and now we were going to move? It felt as though we were aimed in different directions, but I didn't want to be the one standing in Geoff's way, so I reluctantly agreed to the move. We were going to uproot ourselves and our kids from everything we knew and move eleven hundred miles across country. What if this was the biggest mistake of our lives?

As we loaded the moving van, I felt like a spoiled, stubborn three-year-old. My body may have been bending as I got in the car, but my will sure wasn't. I didn't want to uproot my kids. I didn't want to start over with our church and friends and career. The voice in my head told me Geoff was only thinking about himself, not us. I had no words to talk to him about it, and I sure had no words for God.

Steve Jobs said you can rarely see the path looking forward, but in hindsight, the dots become connected, allowing you to see how events have lined up to bring you to where you are.[2] Looking back, I can clearly see God's hand forming our path, but as it was happening, it felt like events were independent of us, spinning out of control. Geoff and I had always felt like partners. What in the world had happened that now made this feel so different? I didn't realize it, but my resentment had been a slow creep. I wasn't talking to anyone: not Geoff, not God, not wise friends.

After we had been in Charleston for several months, I hit bottom. Geoff loved his position as family ministry pastor and was able to use his gifts of teaching and strategic thinking. But I felt lost. One night, after getting up in the middle of the night to console ten-year-old Mike, who was missing his friends in Houston, I decided this wasn't working and I began to plan to pack up the kids and leave. I had no idea where we'd go or what I'd do, but I knew I was done with this. But by morning I had talked myself out of leaving right then; I'd wait until the school year ended to make the transition easier for Mike and Brittainy. I felt this was the end of our marriage.

~

The first few months at Seacoast were the hardest months of my (Geoff's) life. I was in a new role at a new church in a new town. The only people I knew were my brother and my wife. My brother was now my boss, and my wife wasn't speaking to me. Part of my role as family pastor was to teach others how to have a healthy marriage. I felt like a hypocrite telling people how to invest in their relationship while my marriage was slowly unraveling. Sherry and I would go days and say nothing more than a bare minimum of words. I didn't know until later that she was planning on leaving, but I wouldn't have been surprised. And I don't know if I would have tried to stop her. I had allowed bitterness to build so high in my heart that I no longer saw the beautiful young lady I had married fourteen years before. All I saw was resentment.

BEGIN AGAIN

We couldn't see it coming, but God was about to do something big. It was time for Seacoast's annual marriage retreat and guess whose job description it fell under? So we arranged for a babysitter, packed our bags, and headed to Myrtle

Beach to show couples how to work on their marriages while thinking ours was beyond repair.

At the end of the first night of the retreat, another pastor told everyone to stand, take their spouse by the hand, look into their eyes, and tell them how much they loved them. We were on the front row, and it felt like everyone was looking at us. We looked into each other's empty eyes and mouthed the words without meaning. The moment seemed to go on forever, but finally the leader moved on to the next itchy activity. We knew the weekend was going to be torture, but we didn't realize God was just getting warmed up.

Right before lunch the next day the retreat leader announced the entire afternoon was dedicated to free time for the couples. He said we should spend time alone, just the two of us, enjoying each other. This was not good news. For months we had avoided spending time alone together. The tension was so high it was painful to sit in silence, staring at each other across the room. Now we were faced with hours of nothing but alone time. We walked back to our hotel room, flipped on the TV, and sat silently, staring at whatever was on.

As we sat there, I (Sherry) began to feel God break me. I didn't know how to express the inexpressible, the resentment, the unreasonable expectation, and the unspoken thoughts inside, but I realized in that moment that I didn't want to live in the ugliness anymore. I took Geoff by the hand and said, "I want to be your friend." Those six words marked the beginning of a new chapter in our marriage. The resentment and bitterness were not instantly washed away, but the dam finally burst, and for the first time in months we began to talk, to laugh, and to love again. God began to heal us.

We realized we had to learn how to do marriage and ministry together even though we had already been doing it for years. I needed to learn that sometimes ministry is just plain hard work. I had to get comfortable with other people's expectations and unhappiness and not let it eat me up inside. I knew it wasn't my job to make everyone like our church or even like us, and I had to learn how to live it out every day, even when ministry wanted to make me run screaming from the room. These lessons have been years in the making, and they began with a few things I wish I had learned a whole lot sooner.

LESSONS FROM THE EDGE

First, the hard things can become good things. I have always secretly wondered if the writer of James was delusional when he wrote, "When troubles of any kind come your way, consider it an opportunity for great joy" (1:2). He had clearly never encountered Sister G—, who had a penchant for calling before God himself was up on a Sunday morning, just to read me the list of folks who wouldn't be at church that day. After talking to her on the phone, it wasn't joy I was feeling. But the writer goes on to say: "For you know that when your faith is tested, your endurance has a chance to grow. So let it grow, for when your endurance is fully developed, you will be perfect and complete, needing nothing" (vv. 3–4).

That's what I wanted, but it just can't happen without the Sister G—s in my life, no matter how hard I try. If I hang in there and do my part, God will do his, teaching me even through those phone calls that he has enough mercy and forgiveness and love to carry me. He can show me that no matter what people do or say, I'm going to be okay in his big hands. He can help me have just enough self-control for those moments when the people in my church make me want to say bowling words. I wish God would just go ahead and make me perfect, but that's not going to happen. I still have my days when I lose my grip on my sane self, but with each hard moment, when I hang on, I get one step closer to being who God intends me to be.

I've learned (and still am learning) that sometimes the hardest voice in my life is my own. At Church on the Lake, I felt I had to fill in every hole and make everyone happy. Every person who left felt to me like a personal defeat, and when they did, I heard a pushy voice in my head say, "Try harder, do more, and maybe they won't leave." I'm learning to shut down that voice and remind myself that my best is all I can do and my best is enough for God to use.

I've learned what a gift it is to be able to talk to Geoff about the hard stuff and how I'm feeling about it. It's a healing thing to admit when I'm discouraged and to put words to the junk that's going on in my head and heart when ministry feels like a punch in the face. Being honest together about how hard it was—and still is—started with being able to look back and laugh at some of the more ridiculous moments.

Like the time E— hid my store-bought cake in the cabinet at a women's dinner because she was sure I didn't know how to bake and wanted to hide my shame.

Like the time the adult Sunday school class spent twenty minutes discussing how it could be possible for the father of the prodigal son to fall "on his neck" (KJV). "How do you fall down on your own neck?" someone asked. I remember wondering why we were having this conversation.

We laugh about the time between worship leaders when we thought karaoke worship with cassette tapes was a good idea (yep, we really did this, and believe us when we warn others not to try it). I was the one leading worship at the time, and it was incredibly awkward. I remember my brother-in-law Greg coming to our church to visit and asking, "Isn't there *anything* better you could do than that?" At the time, it hurt my feelings, because we really did think it was the best we could do. Now, looking back, I question our sanity.

Sometimes, in the moment, it's too painful to find your

sense of humor. But being able to laugh together is really important. A pastor friend recently told us the story of being in a grocery store after he had given what he thought was a pretty good sermon, and he saw someone from his church. From across the store, loud enough for any to hear, the man yelled, "Hey, Pastor, was that sermon today the best you could do? It was awful!" And he was serious!

It's comments like that that make you want to slit your wrist in the cereal aisle. This pastor said it embarrassed him to pieces, but as he shared it with his wife later, they saw it for what it was. Sometimes people are just obtuse—and funny.

I'm learning in the moment when it feels like your last ounce of hope has drained away, God has more. I love to share this truth with young couples in ministry: You never know what God's got waiting around the next corner. Quitting today might stop God's miracle for tomorrow. Looking back, I know that packing up the kids and leaving Geoff would have been disastrous. It was incredibly selfish and shortsighted. I had no idea the best years were yet to come, but luckily God did. He knew that our family's time at Seacoast Church in Charleston would launch both of our kids into ministry. He knew we'd get opportunities to speak and write together and to encourage other ministry couples. He knew if we'd just hang on, we'd hit the best years of being together.

Maybe that resonates with you as you read this. If you've been in ministry long enough, you have your own war stories. Ministry is working with people, and people are quirky and odd and sometimes downright mean. Ministry means working long hours and it's still never done. And then you get griped at. But it's never God's intention for ministry to throw your marriage or family into a ditch.

Take a minute to take stock of where you are. Have you felt a few nudges as you've read this? Are there things you need to talk about but have never said out loud before? Is there crud you've stuffed down deep that you've never shared with your spouse? Let the questions below guide you into some honest conversation.

TO TALK ABOUT

- How do each of you do in talking about what's causing you pain in ministry? Are there things you resent that you haven't talked to your spouse about? What would you like to say to each other right now?

- If there is resentment, can you identify where it's coming from? Is it from your ministry load, from expectations from your spouse or church, or is the voice from inside you?

- Are you able to look back and laugh about some of the hard moments? If not, how could you get there?

5

Balancing Act

One of the biggest challenges for a family engaged in ministry is learning to balance church activities, marriage, kids, extended family, finances, and all the needy people who seem to come along with the job. Just leading a ministry or a church can be a 24/7 endeavor. Volunteers can't meet during the workday, crises almost always occur in the middle of the night, and weekends are the busiest time for someone in ministry. In the midst of the chaos are recitals, ball games, and graduations, along with all the other needs of a healthy family. Somewhere along the way you're supposed to have family meals, date nights, and vacations. Balancing all this endless activity requires a spreadsheet, a calendar app, and a daily to-do list. And no matter how hard you try, something always seems out of balance. Either ministry or family seems to always get shortchanged. How does anyone successfully balance all the demands of ministry, friends, and family?

The good and bad news is that it is impossible. The idea of a balanced life is a myth, especially for people engaged in significant ministry. No one can give equal amounts of time to the needs of leading a ministry, the demands of people in crisis, and the proper care and feeding of a marriage and a family. This is obviously bad news that balance is unachievable, but it is good news because we are not alone: every ministry family is failing at balance. The reality is that balance isn't even a worthwhile goal.

We do not find balance in the Bible. The apostle Paul was not a balanced guy. He laid everything on the line in ministry, describing his life as "being poured out like a drink offering" (Phil. 2:17).

Jesus did not live a balanced life. He healed the sick, taught the disciples, preached to thousands, and rebuked the Pharisees all in the same day. And he said, "The Son of Man has no place to lay his head" (Luke 9:58). That doesn't sound like a balanced life.

For someone leading at a church, the impossibility of balance becomes acute during the Easter and Christmas seasons.

For good or bad, these two holidays are often treated like twin Super Bowls. This was a major challenge during the early years of our time at Seacoast Church. Every Easter season the church put on an original musical production that included both a contemporary drama and a live depiction of the Passion week. Part of my (Geoff's) role was to lead the writing team and direct the technical side of the performances. I don't know if you've ever written and produced a two-and-a-half-hour musical production, but it can be a bit time consuming. The kicker is that the week of production was always during the kids' spring break. Easter presented an impossible menu of required activities that denied the concept of balance. I'm sure you have many examples of your own. There are times in ministry and marriage that two and two add up to five, and there's no way to balance that equation.

After thirty-plus years of ministry and many seasons of more time demands than we could possibly meet, we are learning that balance can't be our goal. There will always be times when our lives are out of balance, times when ministry, marriage, or family will demand nearly all our time and attention. The goal can't be balance; the goal must be health. While Jesus and Paul did not live balanced lives, they lived healthy lives. Paul was so convinced the life he and Jesus lived was healthy, he invited us to imitate him as he imitated Jesus. We are discovering several keys to a healthy life in the middle of the chaos of family and ministry.

TELL THE TRUTH

Since I grew up in a pastor's home, I (Geoff) was well aware of the time demands of ministry. Everything in our family revolved around the church calendar. All our vacations were planned around church conferences. We didn't play youth sports because that would mean missing midweek church services, and school activities never took precedence over something going on at church. I entered marriage thinking this was normal, and I assumed Sherry and I would raise our family the same way. It never occurred to me that Sherry might have a different picture of a healthy family life. As I slowly became aware she wasn't happy with the idea of letting the church calendar dictate family time, I subconsciously created a strategy to cope with her dissatisfaction. I began to shade the truth about time commitments at church. Rather than talking about upcoming events and creating a plan together, I would simply not talk to Sherry about them. As an event neared, I felt the pressure building until I finally admitted I would be gone on Friday night or this weekend or all next week. Obviously, this didn't lead to the happy, healthy marriage I envisioned.

Telling the truth about time commitments is one of the challenges we continue to face. We don't lie to each other, or at least we pretend we don't lie, we just avoid saying what we are really thinking and feeling about the commitments we've made. Neither of us likes confrontation, so rather than being honest, we sometimes tell little half-truths to keep a semblance of peace.

I (Sherry) am a recovering stuffer-pretender. I'm not sure how I started down this path, but I became really good at it. Things would come up (like Geoff working 24/7 during the kids' spring break), and instead of talking about it, I shoved it deep inside and told myself it didn't matter. I believed to talk about it would make it worse, so I didn't. That's not only unwise, it's dishonest. And I wasn't fooling anyone. While I wasn't saying it in words, I wore my resentment like an ill-fitting coat and I'm sure others (including my kids) could sense it.

I also had issues with underestimating how much time something took and then overcommitting myself. I would say yes to something and then find myself resenting the fact I had taken it on. Sometimes it would come out sideways as resentment toward Geoff, when he resented how much time I was spending on something, and it became a pile of yucky mess I didn't even understand myself.

One of the things Geoff and I are learning to do is to call each other out. We don't just talk about how things are going; we urge the other to talk about how they are feeling about how it's going. Inside. Deep down. Maybe talking about your hidden feelings comes easily for you. It doesn't for Geoff and me. Every morning we start by asking how the other is feeling about their day, and then we pray specifically for each other. Out loud. Geoff wraps his arms around me and speaks words of encouragement and protection over me. (Isn't it weird how we can pray out loud for everyone so easily but our spouse?) At the end of the day we ask each other questions like "Where did you see God at work today?" "What was the hardest part about today and how did you feel about it?" These questions help us to talk about what really matters, namely, how our heart is doing and how it affects our relationship.

After years of conflict around balancing ministry and family, we are learning to simply be honest. We face our fear of confrontation, understand that balance is impossible, and agree to work together to continually create a healthy schedule for our family. These conversations are always challenging and sometimes contentious, but they are the only path to health for our marriage and family.

IDENTIFY THE SEASONS

Early on in marriage it felt like life had two modes: overwhelming and complete insanity. Sherry was finishing college while I (Geoff) was learning how to be a youth pastor–children's pastor–janitor. Sherry began substitute teaching after graduation, and then after our son was born she began teaching full-time. My job became more stressful as the church grew and I took on more responsibility. Then our daughter came along. If life continued like this, it would be unsustainable. Life and ministry, however, never stay the same. As the writer of Ecclesiastes says, "There is a time for everything, and a season for every activity under the heavens" (3:1). Just like everything else in life, ministry, career, and marriage have seasons. One of the biggest keys to finding health in the whirlwind is to identify the natural seasons.

Some have described ministry as a marathon, but it's really a series of sprints with brief rest times in between. Ministry seasons like Christmas, Easter, and summer programs are sprints. Skipping Easter isn't an option, but it's helpful to remember that at the end of the sprint there is a time for rest. If there is never a time for rest and it isn't possible to have a healthy break, it's time to find a different role. Life without seasons is unsustainable.

Life, like ministry, also has seasons. When the kids are young, it seems as if this season will last forever, especially when so much time and effort goes into ministering to other families. We currently have three grandchildren. (We know we keep mentioning the grandkids—we can't help it.) At least once a month the grandkids spend the night with us because we love it and it gives their parents a break. Every visit entails shrieks of joy, tears of despair, and every emotion in between. (And that's just Geoff.) Bedtime is a major production, as are breakfast, lunch, and dinner. By the time the kids go home, we are exhausted, and we're just pinch hitters. Their mom and dad do it every day of the week. I'm sure there are many days our son and daughter-in-law feel like they're stuck in the movie *Groundhog Day* and fear this season will never end. Like all stages of life, however, this season will inevitably change. Eventually the kids will go to school, their finances will improve, and breathing room will return. Someday the parents will look back on this season wistfully, remembering the joy and forgetting much of the exhaustion. And then they will have grandkids.

The key is to recognize the seasons of life and the seasons of ministry and plan around them. When Sherry was the children's pastor at Seacoast Church, I knew the weeks around Vacation Bible School would be crazy every summer. I needed to adjust my schedule to take more of the load with the kids during that season, and the week of VBS wasn't the week to plan a retreat for the other campus pastors. When the kids were young, we didn't have a lot of time for ministry opportunities outside of our regular roles in the church. Now that we are empty nesters, we have the time and margin to speak at conferences, coach other church leaders, and write books. Balance is impossible in the moment; balance is only possible across a lifetime. In the immediacy of every season, healthy rhythm is the goal.

DEFUSE EMERGENCIES

Everything in ministry can feel like an emergency. The sermon has to be ready by Sunday, a new children's ministry volunteer must be recruited before the weekend, and a parishioner's crumbling marriage has to be fixed tonight. All the good intentions of focusing on family go out the window when the phone rings. It's time for all hands on deck to put out the fire. Ministry refuses to wait while you sit around the dinner table, listening to a kindergartner tell knock-knock jokes. Often ministry feels like a series of emergencies coming in unpredictable waves.

The little-known secret of ministry, however, is many emergencies can be delayed, defused, or dealt with in advance. Since weekends come every seven days, things like sermons and song lists can be written days, weeks, or months in advance. One of the most freeing habits I was forced into at Seacoast Church was having to turn in my sermon notes by noon on Thursday so everything could go to the printer. No matter what else happened from Monday to Wednesday, my notes had to be done by noon Thursday, no exceptions. What that meant is the stress of sermon prep was focused on the first half of the week. By Thursday afternoon, for good or bad, the sermon was done. I didn't have to deal with a panicky feeling of impending doom on Friday and Saturday, and by Sunday afternoon the damage was done.

Volunteer recruitment is another emergency that can be planned for. The pressure of finding, training, and deploying ministry partners is an occupational hazard of ministry. We used to think that big churches didn't struggle with volunteers—until we worked at big churches. Now, instead of needing a dozen volunteers every weekend, we need hundreds. In a volunteer-driven environment there will always be times when there simply aren't enough bodies to go around. This shouldn't be an emergency. As a counselor told us when we described the pressure of finding children's ministry volunteers every week: "What's the worst that could happen? A class might not have a teacher, so a child might have to sit with their parents during church." That's not ideal, but it's not an emergency. Since having enough volunteers is a constant need, and not having enough can raise stress levels through the roof, developing new leaders should be the primary task for anyone in vocational ministry. And even in the best of circumstances there will be events without enough volunteers to go around. The key is to build worst-case scenarios and discuss them with leaders and teams in advance. It is only an emergency if you can't predict it can happen and don't prepare in advance in case it does.

When we lived in Houston soon after getting married, we experienced Hurricane Alicia, a Category 3 storm with 135-mile-per-hour winds when it came ashore. As devastating as a Category 3 storm can be, Alicia would have been a relatively minor storm except for one Houston contractor.

His company was completing the roof of a brand-new sky-scraper. As part of the project, several tons of gravel were piled fifty stories above the city. Although there was plenty of warning as the storm approached, the contractor did not properly secure the gravel on the rooftop. When the hurricane arrived, the air was filled with millions of tiny gravel projec-tiles traveling at over 100 miles per hour in every direction. As the gravel shattered the windows of nearby skyscrapers, millions of additional projectiles were created in the form of flying shards of glass. The debris covered the streets for several blocks and shut down dozens of businesses for weeks after the storm. The eventual price tag for Alicia soared past $2.5 billion, making it at that time the most expensive storm in history. Most of that damage could have been avoided by better preparations for an emergency everyone knew was coming. The same is true of much of the damage done by predictable ministry emergencies.

The most challenging emergencies, however, come in the form of unexpected phone calls. A marriage is falling apart, a teenager is off the rails, or there's been a bad report from a doctor. They need to meet with a pastor right now, tonight, after they get off work. It doesn't matter if this is your date night or the night of your ten-year-old's ballet recital, you're expected to drop everything and step into the crisis. As pas-tors and ministers, this is what we do: we step into people's lives at their most vulnerable times and help them connect to the grace and healing of the gospel. As important as family life and marriage are, crisis is where we best fulfill our call to shepherd God's people. The challenging thing is that not all emergencies are truly crises of the moment. Many emergencies are serious but may not require your immediate undivided attention. Here are a few clarifying questions to help differentiate between "drop everything and go" and "let's find a time to get together."

- Did this crisis just arise or is it something that has been brewing for a while?
- Is this a crisis you can solve tonight or will this be an ongoing challenge?
- Is there a compelling reason this crisis can't be addressed during normal business hours?

A crumbling marriage is an example of a crisis that, while serious, is not always urgent. It has likely taken many years to get to this point, and the challenge probably cannot be solved in one Tuesday night session in your living room. If the couple isn't willing to take time off from work to work on their marriage, they may not be ready to seriously address their challenges. In a chronic situation, it's important the couple knows you care and want to help, but you have immediate commitments you cannot get out of tonight, such as a child's ball game, a date night with your wife, or a night as a family. The person on the other end of the phone does not have to know what your commitment is or share the priority you place on your commitment. They simply need to know you are willing to help, but not right now.

Obviously, there are situations when a pastor must drop everything. I remember getting a call on a Sunday morning that a young man who attended our church fell on his child the night before, and the toddler was in intensive care, clinging to life. That was a drop-everything-and-rush-to-the-hospital emergency. In a situation like that, you deal with what is in front of you and sort out the details later. The key is to recognize that not every phone call reaches that level. It takes years of experience to discern the difference between a legitimate crisis that must be addressed immediately and an acute challenge that can wait until tomorrow. The important thing is to know that not every late-night phone call constitutes a legitimate emergency.

The bottom line is that ministry will never be a nine-to-five, Monday-to-Friday job, so creating a healthy rhythm for your family will be a lifelong endeavor. Seasons of imbalance are unavoidable, so you need an action plan to create and maintain a schedule that is healthy for your family. If you don't set your priorities, everyone else will do it for you.

TO TALK ABOUT

- What are the most difficult seasons for your family to find a healthy rhythm?

- Do you have a regular date night as a couple? Do you have family nights? If not, when will you begin a regular rhythm of family time away from ministry?

- Spend a few minutes planning your next over-night getaway or family vacation. What obstacles do you have to overcome to protect this vital time?

6

The Fishbowl

Here we go again, I (Sherry) thought as I strapped our son into his car seat. We were on our way to church with our two-year-old as his wail filled the car: "No! I not wanna go!" I'll be honest, my thoughts echoed his. Mike and I both knew what was coming, and neither one of us wanted to face it. I had to make Mike go into his Sunday school class. I dreaded it. Here we were, the children's ministry leaders, and our own son was throwing a big screaming fit in the hall. "Oh, look, Mike, they have animal crackers," I said in my fake cheerful voice. What I really wanted to do was hiss in his ear, "Look kid, I'll buy you a Mercedes when you're old enough to drive if you'll just take your fingernails out of my arm and stop this screaming."

I know. Bad parenting. But screaming tantrums make me desperate.

Many Sundays after such spectacles of stellar behavior from my kids, I wondered what people thought. Did they expect Geoff and me to be able to raise children who always behaved perfectly with perfect attitudes? Were everyone's eyes on our kids and were they making judgments about our parenting skills based on what they did and said? Were they whispering that I couldn't control my two-year-old? If they were saying that last one, they were dead on.

Eventually I realized while the families in our church were definitely interested in our family habits and parenting style, most weren't judging us. Many of them already knew what I had yet to learn: every family is a unique mess, and while you do your best as parents, ultimately every child grows up to choose his or her own way. I think as parents we give ourselves too much credit when it comes to our children's successes, and we blame ourselves way too much for their failures.

I know now that so many of the things I worried about were truly a waste of time and energy. Would being in a pastor's house make my kids resent church? Would they grow up with a cynical view of people and want nothing to do with ministry? After they left our house, would they choose to have nothing to do with church or, worse, God?

Sometimes this happens, but if you are in ministry with kids in your home, let me set your heart at ease. Raising kids in the ministry can be a great experience, and we learned to lean into the upsides. Our kids loved being "in the know" as far as upcoming church events and plans, and when it was appropriate, we would give them the inside scoop before other people got to hear it. We both led children's ministry at different times, and since we spent a lot of time at church, they knew where the secret stashes of toys and candy were. Mike got a lead acting part in our Kidstuff family production, and Brittainy was on a fast track to playing on the youth worship team, partly because this is where their passion and talents were, but also because they were our kids. We wanted them not to feel like it was just their church but also a place where they could spread their wings and discover who they are. We didn't hesitate to give them opportunities in which we knew they would shine. It was important to us that our kids didn't feel like this was just the place where their parents worked. We wanted church to be as important in their lives as it was in ours.

But we didn't do everything perfectly. We tried not to share our discouragement when the church wasn't growing fast enough or when relationships got difficult, but I'm sure there were times we said things we shouldn't have. We tried not to talk about some difficult people in front of our kids, but sometimes (especially during conversations in the car) we would forget they could hear us. We would get frustrated with our leadership and spew words of discouragement that weren't the wisest. And our kids had front-row seats from which to watch their very imperfect parents.

But I also think we stumbled upon some right things, mostly with the help of others. Here are a few of them.

TIPS FOR THE FISHBOWL

First, we talked a lot about what it meant to be a Surratt. I (Geoff) learned this from my mom when I was growing up in a pastor's home. In my mom's eyes, "pastor's kid" wasn't a job description. She didn't set expectations based on our position in the church or what other people might think. Her expectations were based on her definition of what it meant to be a Surratt. Much of the conversation in our home around the things we did and didn't do was based on this definition. Over and over I heard: "We don't do that. We're Surratts." When I was about eight, I remember wishing I could change my last name. It seemed like the kids named Wood and Brown had a lot more fun. But this fierce loyalty to what our family name stood for stayed with me. When Sherry and I had kids of our own, we created our own definition of a Surratt.

Our kids were raised to believe Surratts don't just go

to church, we do church, which means we serve. While we certainly aren't the most talented people, we believe God wired us with certain passions, and it's our job to find out what they are. We're Surratts, which means we come from a rich heritage of imperfect people who make mistakes, but we also love God with all our hearts. We work. We work hard. We work hard for our church. In talking to our kids, we explained that while going to church isn't an option, how you invest your talent is up to you.

From the beginning, our son loved youth ministry. So even as a middle schooler, he began to volunteer in the youth group, tagging along with the youth pastor, running sound, and playing the bass guitar on the worship team. It was a great experience, and Mike learned firsthand how to plan messy games, how the small group ministry was run, and what was involved in herding a group of noisy middle schoolers. Today, Mike is an executive pastor on staff at a church plant started by his youth pastor, and they have been serving side by side for more than ten years.

Brittainy is musically gifted and taught herself to play the guitar, bass, and drums and started volunteering on the middle school worship team. As a teenager, she took voice and guitar lessons from some of the folks on the church worship team, who influenced her decision to attend a worship intern program at another church. She later joined the staff at Seacoast Church as an audio engineer.

Today, both of our kids work full-time for churches, and

we wish we could say it was due to our stellar parenting. It was more likely the great ministry opportunities that helped them discover who God had wired them to be. They went from watching church to doing church, and the shift helped them to love their church.

The second thing we got right in raising pastor's kids is that we encouraged our kids to sink into the small-group opportunities in the youth group. To be honest, our kids didn't always want to. There was a time when our daughter pushed back on going to her small group that she felt didn't fit her. We explained that finding a small group was like tasting a new kind of pizza. Just because you don't like the toppings, it doesn't mean you swear off food forever. You try another bite or a different pizza or even a different food until you find what suits you.

⁓

Several months later, after Brittainy had found another girls' group, I (Sherry) wandered into her room in search of dirty towels to throw in the washer. I saw pastel-colored cards on the floor by her bed next to her Bible. When I asked her about the cards, she told me her small group leader had shared how she wrote special Bible verses on index cards to keep by her bed. Whenever the leader worried about something at night, she would read the verses and they helped her go to sleep. Brittainy decided she would try it too. This practice came because we chose to partner with the small-group leaders in our church in raising our kids.

When Mike was in ninth grade, I went to pick him up from his group at the youth pastor's house. Usually when I drove up, there were about a dozen boys wrestling or throwing a football around the front yard, but tonight, not a single boy was in sight. Impatient, I sat in the car for ten minutes, thinking about all the things I still needed to take care of at home before I could go to bed. Finally, I marched up to the front door in frustration to ring the bell, but I stopped dead in my tracks. The door was open and I could see about ten boys lying face down on the carpet. Ernest, their youth pastor, was walking around them, praying over them before they left. He prayed, *"Lord, let them grow up to be the godly men you designed them to be. Give them wisdom to say no and courage to say yes. Protect them, Lord, with your mighty hand."* I spun around and sneaked back to my car. I would sit there all night if I needed to. Who cared about laundry when you had a young pastor praying over your teenage son?

We are so thankful for the tremendous influence that being part of a church has had in our kids' lives. We are thankful we somehow had the wisdom to insist that our kids be involved, especially as they grew to be teenagers and didn't always want to. It was tempting to just let them make their own decisions, especially as we worried that insisting would make them turn away. It didn't.

The final thing we got right was probably the best thing

we did regarding raising kids in a fishbowl: we didn't raise our kids alone. Carey Nieuwhof and Reggie Joiner, in their book *Parenting Beyond Your Capacity*, use the phrase "widening the circle." They talk about the gift of partnering with your church to lean into others who can pour into your children's lives.[3] Luckily, we had the sense to do this, because Lord knows we needed it.

When Mike was a baby, he suffered from colic (a term I think means "to drive Mama out of her mind"). His crying fits always seemed to coincide with Sunday evening church (or anything at church), and I would spend most of the service time walking Mike up and down the halls. During one of our walks, I ran into Paulie.

Paulie was a single lady who had never had children, but she had a gift for being with them, kind of like a baby whisperer. She snatched Mike out of my arms, told me boldly to go sit down, and proceeded to rock him to sleep. To sleep! The child who never fell asleep in anyone's arms gave up the fight in about ten minutes, secure in Paulie's arms.

It was an eye-opener. My parents lived far away, and Geoff's mom was battling cancer, so neither side could really help. But we didn't have to be alone when it came to our kids. There were people all around us, just like Paulie, who could help. As our kids grew older, Paulie came over and spent the night at our house so we could get away for a night together. She adopted them as nephew and niece and made them feel special during really busy ministry seasons when we had our hands full. We believe there's a special place in heaven for baby whisperers like Paulie.

As our kids got older, we had other incredible people who poured themselves into our kids. There was Mel, Brittainy's small-group leader who modeled what it's like to live a godly life as a single woman, and Fran, who often had impromptu dinners at her house and didn't care if the house overflowed with kids who brought their friends. At Brittainy's graduation party, Fran brought over a ginormous cake in the shape of a guitar that she had stayed up all night working on. Both of these ladies taught our daughter what it meant to trust God even when you can't see him working, and they prayed for her as she struggled with panic attacks and anxiety.

Mike had Carl, a single dad, who would throw his front door open to dozens of sweaty, smelly middle schoolers and never complained when they left his house with food tracked on the carpet and an empty refrigerator. Mike also had Andrew and Ernest, who led him in youth ministry and taught him how rewarding ministry can be and that it's always more fun with a team.

We didn't lean into these younger, hipper adults because we couldn't parent our kids. We did because ministry is demanding and can wreak havoc in your family if you let it. So we fought back by widening our circle, and we're glad we did.

One of the hardest things about raising kids, especially in a fishbowl like ministry, is finding a template for parenting that fits your family. Several years ago, I (Geoff) was eating lunch with a group of pastors when the conversation turned to parenting. One particularly confident leader described a ritual he took each of his sons through on their thirteenth birthday. I don't remember all the details, but I think it involved a trip to the mountains, a lot of manly oaths, and maybe a goat was sacrificed. (I might have made up that last part.) I was completely intimidated because Mike's thirteenth birthday ritual involved Applebee's and bowling. I always wanted to be a ritual-and-sacrifice dad, but it didn't fit my wiring.

That's the biggest key to raising kids in the fishbowl: you have to be who you are. You can't create an image that looks good to church people but doesn't match your DNA. We decided long ago that we are simple folk. We like to play silly games and tell stupid jokes that no one outside our family thinks are funny. We think sarcasm might just be a spiritual gift, and we exercise it regularly. We are an odd bunch who like to talk about church and ministry strategy at dinner with our kids. We never had structured family devotions, but we took the Shema to heart:

> These commandments that I give you today are to be on
> your hearts. Impress them on your children. Talk about
> them when you sit at home and when you walk along

the road, when you lie down and when you get up. (Deut. 6:6–7)

We talked to our kids about life and decisions and friends and dating in the moments that were right in front of us. In the car, in the bathroom, while shooting free throws on the driveway. We talked about the power of prayer and acknowledged the way God was answering those prayers. We've come to grips with the fact that we're unique, and we don't try to copy anyone else because we wouldn't do it right anyway. We made mistakes with our kids, but then we apologized. We talked about ministry in our home and tried to let it be what it is. Hard. Messy. Incredibly rewarding.

RAISING BOYS IN A FISHBOWL

We asked Geoff's sister, Dee McGarity, about her experience in raising kids in a fishbowl. She and her husband, Doug, have four boys, all born in a span of eight years. Our kids always loved to stay at their cousins' house, because there was always something crazy going on. At one point the McGaritys may have had their own suite in the local emergency room. Somehow in the chaos of raising boys, moving multiple times, and pastoring in a variety of roles, they managed to raise incredible young men who love Jesus with all their hearts. We wanted to know, looking back, the lessons they learned along the way.

The hardest thing about raising the boys in a pastor's home was that our life was so public (Dee). The boys went to school, childcare, and church at the same place where Doug and I worked. Some days the boys would start the day in the church school, go to the after-school program at the church daycare, and finish the day playing on one of the church sports teams. All along the way it felt like people in the church were watching and judging how the boys behaved and how we responded. When the boys misbehaved, we had to be careful to keep our reactions in line with the offense rather than the embarrassment factor. With four young boys in the spotlight, we had plenty of opportunities to practice.

At the same time, people could be overly flattering toward the pastor's kids. Because everyone knew the McGarity boys, they were often singled out for recognition. We had to remind the boys and ourselves that we were big ducks in a very small puddle. We were determined they would not consider themselves above anyone else.

One area I struggled with was creating more separation between our family and our work. Being a pastor is the only job where your social life, school, sports, and everything in-between is tied to your job. Every time Doug moved to a new ministry position, the boys had to go to a new church, adjust to a new youth group, and start over with a new set of friends. This was an incredibly difficult adjustment for the boys, and we didn't always do a great job of preparing them for the transition.

One of the things I tell young couples going into ministry is to keep the negative aspects of ministry out of your home as much as possible. As a pastor, you experience the dark side of many people's personalities, and it's easy to bring that home to your family. You don't want your kids, however, to equate God with misbehaving church members. It is important your kids get a true picture of ministry, but your role as a parent is to protect them from some of the garbage.

LOOKING BACK

Sometimes when we were struggling with our two kids, it gave us perspective to know that Geoff's sister had twice as many kids to deal with—and they were all boys. We get tired just thinking about it. Now as grandparents looking back, we have the unique perspective that you may not have: When your baby needs her diaper changed, the three-year-old is lying on the floor screaming, and the six-year-old just used the safety scissors to give the lead elder's granddaughter a haircut, it's hard to see how you'll survive, let alone thrive as a family in ministry. But trust us, it's going to be all right. Here are five simple principles, based on what we've shared from our experience, to keep your family on track.

1. *Create a family identity*: Take time to think through the things you want your kids to know about being a member of your family. Not a simple list of dos and don'ts, but a description of the mission, vision, and values that make you the unique family God created. If your kids are old enough, include them in the process and refer back to this definition regularly. A strong family identity prevents others from deciding what your family should be.

2. *Fiercely defend your family*: The church doesn't get to decide what your family is and isn't; you do. In ministry there will always be others who will tell you what you should be doing or saying and even what your kids should look and act like. But the ball is in your court. Don't serve it up to anyone else. You decide what your family's boundaries are and what's best for your kids. Give your kids the freedom to discover who God designed them to be and what their relationship with the church and God will look like.

   You are the only champion your family has. Many people in and out of the church have a picture of who your family should be and how your kids should act, but it is your responsibility to stick to the unique picture you're creating. God specifically chose you to raise your kids; only you can decide how they should be raised.

3. *Make ministry a win*: As I (Geoff) look back on growing up in a pastor's home, the best thing my parents did was encourage us to serve in ministry. I hated Sunday school and I got kicked out of children's church, but I loved volunteering in the puppet ministry. I think my experience in volunteering as a teenager is the biggest reason I am still involved in ministry today, and I've seen my children have the same experience. As a leader in the church, you have the opportunity to help your kids find a place they love to serve.

4. *Partner with others*: Help your kids connect with adults who will love them, warts and all. They need a safe place where they aren't the pastor's kids, they're just kids. Small-group leaders, youth leaders, or coaches will help your kids discover who they were created to become outside the pressure of ministry. Much of the credit for our children's spiritual walk as adults belongs to the leaders they leaned into when they were young.

5. *Relax*: Ministry can be incredibly difficult, but the kids are going to be okay. As parents, we are called to love, listen to, and guide our children, but in the end, they will find their own path. That is scary for those of us who are control freaks, but it's also comforting. God has our children in the palm of his hand. He is their guide, their protector, and their

rock. Lean into Solomon's wisdom: "Start children off on the way they should go, and even when they are old they will not turn from it" (Prov. 22:6).

What you do at church is important, but it's not the most important thing you'll do. Love your family well. Give your best time to them. At the end of every day, put the church concerns aside and have moments of ridiculous fun when your kids get to see who you really are. In your home, don't be the pastor or ministry leader. Be the best mom and dad you can be.

TO TALK ABOUT

- What are your biggest concerns about raising kids in a minister's home? What is the root of these concerns?

- What are the core values of your family? How do you communicate these values to your children?

- What other adults are involved in the lives of your children? Who else could you lean into or partner with in raising your kids?

7

Pressure Cooker

I (Geoff) didn't really understand the pressure of ministry until I began pastoring a tiny church in rural Texas. Until then I was on staff at a larger church where I didn't have to sweat the budget, count the cars, or pray the air-conditioning units would hold up for one more summer. When I became the lead (and only) pastor, however, all that changed. Now I was the guy responsible for figuring out how we were going to keep the doors open.

Attendance was an immediate and constant pressure

from the day I became the pastor. We began with eleven adults and we never saw an explosion of growth. We would grow by ten, shrink by twelve, and then grow another six. Before Sunday morning services I would pace back and forth in the empty auditorium, stopping every few minutes to peek out the blinds, trying to will cars to turn into the parking lot. I was elated when a family with five kids joined the church, and then depressed whenever they went on vacation. We counted every man, woman, child, and pet who attended. We counted people who only turned around in the parking lot. When we finally grew to fifty people, we held a party with a cake inscribed with "We busted the 50 barrier." I tried not to focus so much on attendance, but it's hard not to notice empty pews from the platform. For a few months we made everyone sit on one side of the auditorium to make it seem like we had more people. I may have overdosed on growth strategy.

Budget was another form of tremendous pressure. Our annual budget averaged sixty thousand dollars our first couple of years. The previous pastor had depleted the church's savings before he left, so every offering was crucial to our survival. Every Monday we wondered if we would be able to pay that week's bills. One particularly bleak January, Walter, the top tither in the church and the father of five, told me his family was moving back to Tennessee "now that the church is doing so well." Our second biggest giver decided to go back to the church he formerly attended, and the third most generous family took offense at our youth director and quit. Within a span of three weeks, 25 percent of our meager budget walked out the door. Since Sherry and I were the fourth biggest tithers, this was a major crisis. If one of the original eleven members had not tithed on their disability settlement at the beginning of February, that would have been the end of the church. When the church finally began to grow, the finances improved, but the financial pressure never let up.

Rounding out the big three of constant pressures was the unrelenting need for volunteers. When we began pastoring, there were two "musicians" in the church: a rhythm-challenged drummer and a pianist who only played songs from a hymnal. One Saturday night our pianist called and said she wouldn't be at church in the morning, which meant our worship band was a drummer. Without a piano player or a clue what to do, I drove to a local Christian bookstore and found accompaniment tapes (they're like MP3s made of plastic) of four songs. That Sunday we did karaoke worship and decided it was significantly better than the band. The next week the pianist and her husband quit—18 percent of the original congregation. Things were moving in the wrong direction.

Pastoring Church on the Lake was not all bad. We saw families restored and people's lives radically changed by the gospel. I learned more about pastoring and leadership in two and half years there than I'd learned in ten years of prior ministry. But the pressure never let up. As I have had the opportunity to work with churches of every size, I've learned the size of a congregation doesn't change the level of the pressure. In larger churches there's pressure to fill the multimillion-dollar auditorium, pressure to meet payroll for dozens of employees, and pressure to fill hundreds of volunteer roles every weekend. Whether you lead in a large ministry, a small ministry, or something in-between, the pressure cooker can be devastating to a marriage.

CHURCH PLANT PRESSURE

Our friends Connie and Shawn Woods planted Freedom Church not far from Charleston, South Carolina, in August 2011. The church has grown rapidly, as has their family; they have four children under the age of twelve as well as one or more foster children most of the time. We asked Shawn and Connie how they handle the pressure of ministry, family, and marriage.

When I (Shawn) was on staff at a megachurch, I felt that I was all in, but there was always a "they" to fall back on. "They" made a decision. "They" are worrying about the finances. "They" will figure out why the church isn't growing. And "they" will fix it. When we planted Freedom Church, I suddenly realized I was "they." The pressure increased for us because we decided to start a church, have a child, build a house, and start the process of being foster parents all at the same time. Fortunately, the church we planted has become a village to help.

The biggest pressure points at the church for me come from my primary roles of preaching, leading the staff, and managing the finances. Preaching a fresh message forty-two weekends a year to a diverse audience, leading a small, stretched staff with the normal share of interpersonal and growth issues, and handling the financial demands of a growing church are always on my to-do list. For Connie the pressure comes from managing relationships, setting boundaries, and being involved in the way God has called her, all with grace, love, and encouragement.

Dealing with Pressure

One of the main ways we deal with pressure is to fiercely protect family time. We have dinner together as a family at least four times a week, and we say no to events that interfere with family dinners or game nights. We take time to pray and discover our mission as a family, not just the mission of the church. We also "date" our kids. The kids especially look forward to their once-a-year night away with their mom and dad. We recognize there are busy ministry seasons, and we plan for them, but we also strategically plan our calendars to prioritize time as a family. And we limit the number of visitors we have at the house. We want our house to feel like a home rather than a church office.

We also prioritize our time together as a couple. We

protect our date night and use babysitting often. We get away as a couple at least twice a year for overnights and usually for a longer trip as well. Early on in planting the church we identified a young lady who helps Connie with the kids and managing things around the house. My assistant also serves Connie, although Connie is not officially on staff. We have built a village to help us on all sides because we can't, and shouldn't, do it alone.

We are also strong believers in preventive counseling. We go to a marriage counselor at least once a quarter. It is important as we carry the burdens of others to be able to process everything that goes into marriage and ministry with someone outside the situation. We also lean into another ministry couple at another local church. It is refreshing to be able to laugh, cry, and pray with someone else who is going through similar circumstances.

Advice for New Ministry Couples

One of the biggest things we've learned is to not take on the burden of feeling like it's all about us. We don't have to convince everyone to come back to church or be friends with everyone. We don't have to accept every invitation to dinner. It's not up to us to make people serve, stay, or attend church. We see couples give up date nights because they "have to" go with a new couple in the church. Don't do it. If it's meant to be, thank God, it's not up to us.

We all have unique pressures in our ministries and marriages, and we all cope with them in different ways. As we wrap up this chapter, let's look at four universal principles for dealing with the pressure cooker of ministry.

1. *You are not alone*: While your stories are different from ours, if you have been in ministry for any amount of time you can relate to the pressures. It is helpful to know that everyone feels the pressures. The church planter who just launched three weeks ago and the megachurch pastor who has been pastoring for thirty years both feel the same kind of pressures you feel. They both struggle with their budget. They both worry about how many people attend or no longer attend the church. They both wonder how they are going to find the leaders they need to fulfill the vision they believe God has given them. When Elijah complained to God that he was the only faithful one left in Israel, God told him there were seven thousand others. Even though Jezebel still wanted Elijah dead, he had to feel great relief in knowing he was not the only faithful one. If you and your spouse are struggling with the overwhelming pressures of doing ministry, know that you are not alone.

2. *Connect with other ministry leaders*: One of the healthiest things we've experienced in ministry is getting together with other ministry couples to

share stories. When we were at Saddleback Church in California we would have all of the campus pastors and their spouses over to our house to just hang out. Before the evening was over, one campus pastor would tell a horrendous volunteer story or a spouse would tell something outrageously rude an attender told them. Other pastors and spouses would chime in with their own fears, challenges, and worries. Inevitably, by the end of the evening, we were laughing, crying, and connecting deeply with one another. You need at least one other couple in ministry to connect with. A couple who can relate to the pressures you feel. You need a couple you can be transparent with, without fear of whom they will tell or what they will think. Trying to survive the pressure cooker alone is a recipe for disaster.

3. *Change the scorecard*: I (Geoff) met recently with a friend who planted a church in Denver, one of the toughest places on the planet to start a new church. His church is already self-sustaining, experiencing growth, and transforming lives. But the pastor is discouraged because the rate of growth is much slower than he expected. Other churches in the area are growing faster, ministries he's led in the past have experienced exponential growth, but he can't figure out what he is doing wrong. Although he said he feels like "God is smiling" on what they are

doing, he feels a great deal of pressure because the church growth isn't measuring up to his perception of success.

Many of us can relate to how he feels. We read on Twitter of dozens committing their lives to Christ and hundreds being baptized while we're seeing incremental growth at best. We don't want to be envious or discouraged, but it feels like an occupational hazard. One of the most spiritual things some us can do is unfollow pastors who make us feel discouraged. It's not their fault; they are just excited about what is happening in their church. But if hearing their "praise reports" isn't helpful, then it's time to cancel the subscription.

We need to change the scorecard of ministry success. We will always pay attention to things like attendance, baptisms, and offerings, but those can't be the measure of our effectiveness in ministry. There's a fascinating glimpse of this in the book of Acts. In chapter 8 we meet an incredible minister named Philip as he is preaching in Samaria. People are committing their lives to Christ, demons are being cast out, and lives are being healed. Can you imagine Philip's Twitter feed blowing up during the Samaritan revival? Philip leaves Samaria and finds himself sharing Christ with a high-ranking Ethiopian official. After the official accepts Christ and is baptized in water, Philip disappears. We don't hear another word about him until an intriguing verse thirteen chapters later: "Leaving the next day, we reached Caesarea and stayed at the house of Philip the evangelist, one of the Seven. He had four unmarried daughters who prophesied" (Acts 21:8–9).

Apparently, Philip spent the majority of his ministry in one city and reared four daughters who loved Jesus and were also called into ministry. By the numbers, Philip's ministry was a failure compared to Peter and Paul, but he raised a great family and left an enduring legacy. Philip changed the scorecard and stayed faithful to what God called him to do, which relates to the fourth aspect we've discovered in dealing with the pressure cooker of ministry.

4. *Remember your first love*: This principle was driven home again recently. I attended a meeting where others were sharing stories of incredible life change happening within their areas of ministry. One children's leader told of a significant breakthrough with the family of a child with special needs after years of frustration, another leader talked about seeing God's healing power in a family who lost their father to suicide, and a third related the story of a woman who recently stepped out of the sewer of life into a new relationship with Jesus. As they shared I realized how removed I've become from the reason

I got into ministry in the first place. I have focused on strategy, structure, and services to the exclusion of shepherding God's flock. I felt something break inside, and I knew I had to get back to the place where I first felt compelled to become a minister.

It is natural to be overwhelmed by the pressures of doing ministry in the pressure cooker of numbers and expectations. The urgency of filling volunteer rolls, developing leaders, and meeting budgets overshadows the sweetness of seeing someone experience the freedom of the gospel for the first time or the fiftieth time. In Revelation, the apostle John commended the Ephesian ministers for their hard work and perseverance, for hitting their numbers. They were doing all the right things, but they were doing it out of obligation rather than thankfulness. John reported: "You have forsaken the love you had at first. Consider how far you have fallen! Repent and do the things you did at first" (2:4–5).

When we feel overwhelmed from dealing with the pressures of ministry, when we find ourselves focusing on church but neglecting our family, when we realize our spiritual tank is empty, it is time to step back and rediscover the passion and call that brought us into ministry in the first place.

TO TALK ABOUT

- What three or four areas cause the most pressure for you? Why are these areas pressure cookers?

- What are some of the positive and negative ways you have handled ministry pressure as individuals and as a couple?

- What is one specific action step you will take to mitigate the impact of ministry pressures on your marriage and family?

8

Church Chat

Sherry and I have both been involved in ministry since we were teenagers. I was on the children's ministry puppet team (as a puppeteer, not a puppet), and Sherry was a leader in the children's choir. There has never been a day since we met that we weren't knee deep in volunteer or vocational ministry, so our conversation always involves something about church. The challenge is that church and nothing but church can be monotonous and overwhelming. This became a major problem for us when Sherry became the children's ministry pastor at Seacoast while I was one of the executive pastors. Sherry had always volunteered in the church while working somewhere else; now we were working together, volunteering together, and living together.

At one point Sherry's office was next to mine, with a window in-between. At random times during the day, she would tap on the window just to say hi. For a brief period, Sherry even reported to me. While this was not an ideal arrangement, it was beneficial at review time: "Mama needs a raise 'cause Daddy needs a new car." (That never happened. Salaries were set by human resources.)

But this was a very exciting time in ministry. Seacoast was growing very quickly, and we were both serving in areas we loved. I oversaw the multisite ministry, identifying campus pastors, finding new locations, launching campuses, and leading the pastors who led the existing sites. Sherry oversaw the development of children's ministry at each new campus and coordinated children's ministry across existing sites. The challenge and growth of ministry was intoxicating. Over the span of five years we grew from three thousand attenders on one site to over eight thousand across eight campuses. We talked about church at work, at home, on date nights, and in bed before we fell asleep. We both loved what we were doing, but we were drowning in church. We had to find an escape. So we bought a boat.

NO SEACOAST ZONE

There's a saying among boat owners that if you want to know what it's like to own a boat, throw your wallet in a lake, but our boat became our respite from church. We bought a used fishing boat and took it out on the tidal creeks around Charleston. We declared the boat a "No Seacoast Zone." When our feet touched the bottom of the boat, all church chat was banned. No talk about service planning, volunteer recruitment, or frustration with staff members. And we gave each other permission to call a time-out any time the church came up in conversation. This led to some pretty quiet boating trips; we didn't have much else to talk about.

One evening we decided to eat dinner on the boat and watch the sunset. There is nothing more beautiful than watching the sunset on the tidal creeks around Charleston: dolphins play in the river, bait fish hit the surface of the water, osprey swoop and call out in the sky above. The evening was perfect. After we finished our sandwiches and the sun sank below the horizon, a chilly breeze began to blow. It was time to pull in the anchor and head for home. It was then I realized I had misread the tide chart. One of the most important things about boating in tidal creeks is knowing how to read a tide chart. At high tide, there is plenty of water to navigate the creeks; at low tide a boat will run aground. Once a boat is beached, the only thing to do is wait for the tide to come back in. Instead of the tide coming in while we ate, it had been going out. When I tried to start the motor, mud shot out the exhaust port, a sure sign we were sitting on the bottom. We had several hours ahead of us, sitting in a chilly wind, waiting for enough water to float our boat. And we couldn't talk about Seacoast. While this is an evening I'd prefer to never repeat, it was actually very refreshing. We faced a crisis that had nothing to do with church attenders, budgets, or volunteers. We talked about our relationship, the kids, and my inability to comprehend a tide chart—something mariners had understood since the time of Christ. We huddled together shivering, laughing, and praying we wouldn't freeze or starve (very remote possibilities) before our boat floated. Eventually, just as it does twice every day, the tide came in and we made it safely home.

FINDING BALANCE

Too much church chat may not be a challenge for you. Hopefully you will set healthy boundaries, maintain outside interests, and engage in healthy conversation around a variety of stimulating topics. A great example of this is our friends Stacy and Andy Wood. They started Southbay Church eight years ago in Silicon Valley, and they've seen incredible growth in an area where new churches seldom survive. The Woods have three kids: ten, eight, and three.

Andy is the lead pastor while Stacy has a variety of roles. They serve as mentors to other ministry couples inside and outside their church. This is what they told us.

Most of our conversations seem to revolve around our kids and ministry (Andy). Part of this is because we both love what we do, and honestly, Stacy is one of the wisest people I know. She always has great insights and is also very passionate about the work. Sometimes we make a conscious choice to talk about something else, but a lot of the time it comes back to ministry. When I'm not bringing up ministry to her, it often feels like she brings up the church to me.

⁓

Honestly, I (Stacy) really love hearing what's going on in the ministry and talking with Andy about it. Andy does a great job of valuing my perspective and asking for my input, which helps me feel very much a part of the team. There have been a few occasions where a specific stressful situation with the ministry has circled around and around our conversations for months, like an airplane that just won't land. I do get worn out by those conversations, and I'm honest with Andy about it. I try to frame it in a life-giving way, for example: "Babe, I've noticed that this is weighing you down so much. You've been talking with me a lot about it. I want you to feel like you can always come to me, but I also want to encourage you to trust God in this situation. I think it could be good to make a conscious decision to draw some boundaries in your own mind about how you want to think about this. What part of this is your responsibility and what is God's responsibility? How can I help you trust God with this?" If I say this to Andy at the right time and with a humble attitude that wants to help, he always receives it as a gift.

Creating boundaries

One of the boundaries we've created is putting our phones aside and turning off technology during the window between when we get home from work and the kids' bedtime. We also do a date night about three times per month. And we aim to take two trips per year, just the two of us. On these trips we do things that get our attention off ministry, such as an outdoor adventure, catching a Broadway show (a perk of living in a big city), or trying out a new restaurant. These trips are so hard to pull off; childcare is a huge barrier, traveling costs a lot of money, and the timing is never convenient. But it has been perhaps the single greatest rejuvenator of our love for one another. You look over at your spouse zip-lining or paddleboarding beside you and think: *Wow, I really like you. I have fun with you. I want to spend the rest of my life with you!*

Advice for others

The best advice we have for other ministry couples is to make sure you do things together. Go to events together, have hobbies together, and as much as possible work on your friendship with each other. This requires intentionality and planning. We have had some bad seasons when the kids were younger, and we spent almost a year working in counseling through some of the stuff we've discussed here. After doing it the wrong way a good portion of our marriage, we have learned we have to make it top priority after our personal pursuit of Jesus. And then, when you get it wrong, learn, confess, and make midcourse adjustments. None of us are going to get it perfect, but we can keep getting better.

CREATING A CHURCH-FREE ZONE

Like Andy and Stacy, we have had our ups and downs in dealing with too much church chat. Balancing budgets, shepherding members, and writing life-changing sermons every seven days can drain the energy needed to keep communication with your spouse vital. If you're like the Woods and us, you need help curbing the church chat. Here are several practical ideas that may be helpful.

1. *Throw the "illegal use of chat" flag:* Anywhere can be a "No Church Zone." You might ban church chat from the bedroom, the dinner table, or just while you're on a date. The key is to give permission for your spouse to call you out when you violate the

ban, and if you care at all about ministry, you will cross the line at some point. We still violate our "No Church Zone" all the time. Just like my car almost steers itself to Dairy Queen for an Oreo Blast (so good), I easily drift into talking about church. When we are in a "No Church Zone" and one of us starts talking shop, the other will say something like, "That's fifteen yards for illegal chatting."

Of course, there are times you need to talk about what is happening in ministry; one of the worst things a ministry leader can do is shut their spouse out of the work they feel passionate about. Many evenings will be filled with discussion around new initiatives at church, the coming weekend services, or the mess of working with people. Talking through church issues is healthy, but only in moderation. Sherry and I will often set aside times when we purposefully focus on what is going on in ministry because it is almost impossible to focus on anything else. We find it important, however, to make this the exception. Otherwise we're back in the same old rut of myopically focusing on ministry. One of us has to throw the "illegal use of chat" flag.

2. *Discover your tidal creek*: For us, boating on tidal creeks provided an escape from the church world, but we had to sell the boat when we moved from South Carolina. Now that we live in Colorado, we

have discovered the joy of hiking in the mountains. Sometimes we'll walk for miles without talking, and at other times we'll talk the entire hike. It is our chance to get away from the house and the pressure of ministry to simply enjoy God's creation and each other. Every ministry couple needs a tidal creek or a mountain path or some other easy place to escape together.

Your tidal creek might be playing a sport together, going to football games, or watching the kids' soccer matches. Some of our friends love to check out garage sales on Saturday mornings, and others simply sit on their porch and watch the neighborhood kids play in the street. It doesn't matter what you do, but it is incredibly helpful to find an activity you both enjoy that has nothing to do with church or ministry. The key, however, is to throw the "illegal use of chat" flag early and often. It's not a tidal creek if you bring the congregation along.

3. *Broaden your circle*: We have mentioned this before, but one of the healthiest things a ministry couple can do is find a circle of friends who have nothing to do with their ministry. They may be in the church or they may not attend church at all, but they aren't involved in any way with your work. More important, they aren't looking to you to fix them, teach them, or respond to their agenda. We

spend so much time helping people, we can become completely drained. We need friends who are simply friends.

I believe this is why Jesus was such good friends with Mary, Martha, and Lazarus. It seems that, while they did learn from Jesus, mostly they just enjoyed being together. I can imagine Jesus dropping by Bethany for a good home-cooked meal, catching up on the local news, and just hanging out. Maybe Lazarus was a carpenter too, and Jesus spent time in his shop trading blueprints and techniques. Imagine learning a better way to build a chair from the one who formed the Rockies. Obviously, we don't really know the nature of their relationship, but we do know Jesus enjoyed being in their home.

Sherry and I often find this experience in small groups. We always look for a small group of people who like us but don't expect too much of us. One of the best groups we've been in met at our next-door neighbor's house when we lived in California. The day we moved in, they invited us to join them the following Tuesday evening. Since we didn't know anyone in town, we decided to check it out. We never missed another Tuesday. It was the quirkiest group we'd ever met. There were single moms and empty-nest couples. There were people with significant resources and people barely able to pay their rent.

Some attended the church where I worked and some did not. The best part was no one expected anything from us; they accepted us instantly and acted like we were their long-lost relatives. Sometimes we would show up early and eat dinner with the host family, and sometimes we would show up late and simply join in the prayer time. It was incredible to just love people who loved us back and expected nothing in return.

It was hard to leave that small group when we moved to Colorado, but we've found other ministry couples here who do not attend our church. It is fun to get together and laugh or cry over the scars ministry can leave. We're not trying to fix, lead, or heal each other; we're simply connecting with another couple who understands what it's like to do ministry for a living. We can't stress how important it is to find other life-giving couples.

You can't allow ministry to smother you. Sharing the redeemed life with people far from God and leading them to be disciples should be life-giving. When you find yourselves feeling overwhelmed, tired, and on the edge of burnout, it's time to retreat from ministry for a few hours and reconnect with each other and with nonneedy friends.

4. *Protect your spouse*: There is a tension in ministry between sharing with your spouse and protecting

them from harm. Sometimes at the end of a tough day of ministry I need to tell somebody about the crazy stuff I've just been through: the stupid thing a staff member did, the cutting remark from an elder, the counseling session with a couple in crisis. The challenge is that when I dump all of this on my wife, I may feel better, but she now has this load of garbage to handle. And she doesn't have the context or the opportunity to work through the situations I shared. Her feelings toward the staff member, elder, or couple are now tainted by conversations she didn't have and conflicts she can't resolve. It is important to share the burden of ministry without drowning our spouse in the mess.

TO TALK ABOUT

- How do you feel about the balance of communication in your family? Is it church heavy, church light, or just right?

- Where are the tidal creeks in your relationship? Where do you go to escape the pressures of ministry?

- Do you have a circle of friends you do life with? If not, what steps can you take to find or create a circle?

9

Healthy Change

Twelve years after moving to Charleston from Houston (see chapter 4), I (Geoff) began to feel that my time at Seacoast was drawing to a close. This was a challenging feeling. I loved Seacoast, and my most fruitful years of ministry had been here. We formed lifelong friendships in the church, and our kids were deeply rooted in the low country. How could we leave a place we loved so much? I was reluctant to share the stirring I felt with Sherry, because the last move had been so excruciating. It was hard to imagine doing it again. I knew, however, if God was stirring my heart, he was stirring Sherry's too, so I decided to see what she was feeling. Sherry confirmed that she, too, was feeling that a change was coming. We had no idea what the change might mean, and we were scared to death, but we began to pray and listen for what God was saying.

After a few weeks, we both felt certain the curtain was closing on our current ministry roles at Seacoast, so I decided to talk with my brother Greg, the lead pastor at Seacoast. I told him how much I loved my time and role at Seacoast and how grateful I was for the incredible opportunities I had been given. And then I said that as much as I loved Seacoast and Charleston, I felt God was moving me to my next assignment. Greg was incredibly gracious, saying he had hoped we would continue to work together for many years, but if this was God's timing for a change, he would do anything in his power to help us find our next role in ministry.

The wheels were in motion, and now it was time to discover our new adventure. I was excited about what doors would open. Would I become lead pastor at an existing church? Would I find a role as an executive pastor at another growing church? Would we stay in the Southeast or would we relocate to another part of the country? The anticipation of change was exciting and frightening at the same time. I felt certain a new chapter would begin soon, but nothing happened. No calls, no offers, no opportunities. Just silence.

After several months of waiting and hoping, a church in

Atlanta invited us to interview for the lead pastor role. We liked the church and the area, and we seemed to connect with the elders. We began to feel this might be the right fit. A couple of weeks later they asked me to come back alone and interview again. Once again there seemed to be a connection. On my way to the airport to fly home, I called Sherry and said I was pretty sure this was where God was leading us. She agreed that she was feeling a peace about making this move. We began to think about what it would be like to lead a church in the northern suburbs of Atlanta.

Two weeks later the lead elder called. He said, "Geoff, we appreciate your time, but we don't feel you are the right candidate to lead our church. I wish you well and will be praying for your family."

"Thanks for letting me know," I said.

"You bet, thanks for your time," he said. "Good-bye."

One year into our search for my next ministry role, my only opportunity ended with a two-minute phone call. I said all the right things about closed doors being a comfort and being relieved that the wait was over, but inside the rejection was incredibly painful.

And the waiting continued.

The next opportunity came in the form of a random phone call from a pastor I knew well by reputation; in fact, I was a fanboy. I was so nervous talking to one of my ministry heroes on the phone I was almost incoherent. He asked if I was interested in flying to California to interview for the job of executive pastor at his church. *Are you kidding me? I've been dreaming about this day all my life!* We set a date, and a few weeks later Sherry and I boarded a plane to the job of a lifetime. I still couldn't believe it. I was not only going to meet this amazing leader but I might even work with him.

We were in California for four days and sat through over twenty-five individual interviews. We met with every staff member, every elder, and several well-known people in the community, including a vice president of a giant tech company (which shares its name with a fruit) and the head of one of the most prestigious search firms in the country. It was the most extreme vetting process I'd ever experienced. By the time we boarded a plane back to the East Coast our heads were spinning. As Sherry and I compared notes on the flight home, however, we both knew that it wasn't a fit. Although we loved the community, the church, and the people we met, I wasn't the right person for the job. One of the hardest phone calls I have ever made was calling a man I have incredible respect for to tell him I couldn't come work for him.

Eighteen months into our search and we were 0–2. I think the leaders at Seacoast were beginning to wonder if I would ever leave. I was like the uncle who comes for Thanksgiving and stays for Christmas.

A few months after stepping away from the "opportunity of a lifetime," I received a call from another church in California. Once again, the church was led by one of my ministry heroes. They were looking for someone to oversee their church plant strategy and multisite campuses. Was I interested? I was excited about the possibility but feeling a little gun-shy after the first two disappointments. Sherry and I talked and agreed I should at least explore the opportunity.

Their executive pastor and I were both going to be at a conference in Las Vegas in a couple of weeks, so we agreed to talk there. The executive pastor suggested we talk at the end of the first day's activities, which turned out to be midnight local time and 3:00 a.m. by my East Coast body clock. I had the biggest ministry interview of my life in a Las Vegas hotel lobby when my mind and body thought it was 3:00 a.m. I have no idea what he asked or what I answered, but two weeks later Sherry and I were in California and meeting with one of the most famous pastors in America and his staff. Two weeks after that we agreed to move to California and take the newly formed role. In the span of two months we'd gone from wondering if we would be in limbo forever to working at one of the highest profile churches in the country.

Making the decision to move was one of the toughest things we'd encountered in our marriage. We still had the scars from the last move, and we were leaving a place we both loved. To make it even more difficult, our oldest son and his wife had just given birth to our first grandbaby—and they lived in Charleston. We were leaving our church, our friends, and the most beautiful granddaughter on earth. With heavy hearts as well as anticipation of a new adventure, we loaded everything we owned and moved twenty-five hundred miles to Southern California. Although we missed everything we left behind, we were confident we were following God's lead into our next chapter of ministry.

WHAT CHANGED

It was fourteen years between our move to Charleston and our move to California. On the outside the move to California seemed more challenging; we were moving to a place where we knew no one while leaving our kids and grandbaby behind. The move to Charleston had almost ripped our marriage apart, but the move to California brought us closer together. During the fourteen years in Charleston, while we worked on repairing our marriage and rebuilding our relationship, we learned a lot about change and how to do things differently. Here are several of the things we learned.

1. *We talked it through*: Once Sherry agreed to move to Charleston, we stopped discussing the move. We talked about logistics and the practical steps we had to take, but we didn't talk about how we felt, our misgivings, or our fears. Sherry didn't want to talk about it, and I didn't want her to back out. I felt like the move was the right next step, so what else was there to talk about?

In contrast, we discussed the move to California from every angle. We talked about leaving our family, selling a house we loved, and moving to a city where we had no friends. We gave each other permission to veto the move anywhere along the path. We were honest about our excitement and our misgivings, which led to a much healthier transition. Because we were transparent in our communication, there weren't any huge surprises along the way.

2. *We sought outside counsel*: When we were considering moving to Charleston, we kept it to ourselves. Not only were we not talking to each other about the positives and negatives of making a huge change, we weren't talking to anyone else either. We were making one of the biggest decisions of our lives, and we were making it in a vacuum. Looking back, we realize the foolishness of approaching such a change alone. But our relationship was so raw and full of pent-up emotion, we were afraid to let others see the mess we were creating.

Fourteen years later we talked to everyone we knew about the transition. We asked friends, family members, and casual acquaintances to weigh in on the decision. We even talked to complete strangers. We wanted everyone's opinion. One of the most affirming moments in the process came in the form of an unexpected phone call from a close relative saying they felt strongly we were making the right choice. We never expected that call, it wasn't the kind of input we'd ever received from this relative, and we took it as a sign that God was speaking directly to us. Along the way we received many affirmations as well as great ideas about how to better think through our choices.

3. *We went in knowing there were no guarantees*: As we approached our first move I tried to assure myself—and everyone else—that everything was going to turn out great. We would love the new church, the new state, and the new culture we were walking into. We would find a great neighborhood with great schools, and our kids would have great friends. I didn't have a clue if any of this would work out, but I wanted it to be true. I did everything I could to control everyone's emotions so we wouldn't have to deal with the messiness of a major life change. Eventually we did love the church, the state, and the culture, but it was years in the making. In the short term, we were miserable. The reality of change is that it often starts with much pain.

As we approached the move to California we knew there were no guarantees. Everything might turn out great or we might be walking into the most challenging thing we would ever face. We saw the lack of certainty as part of the adventure of beginning a brand-new life. We knew there were no guarantees, but we were following God by faith and seeing how it would go. It was extremely scary, but it was a much healthier approach to change. We'd learned that change always involves a great deal of uncertainty, and that's okay.

I'd love to tell you that once we learned to engage healthy change in marriage everything got way better. We were finally past the waiting stage, wondering what might be next. We talked the decision through with each other, we sought outside counsel, and we stepped out in faith. We followed all the right steps and moved forward in unity, so the outcome obviously would be great. While that would be the best way to end the chapter, unfortunately it wouldn't be accurate.

Within a few weeks of arriving in California I realized I had stepped into the most difficult ministry experience of my life. I was in way over my head in the area I was leading, the church culture we entered was wildly different than the culture we left, and the job I was asked to do was not at all the job I thought I was being hired to do. I had led us to leave everyone we loved and everything we knew, and now I was miserable. The misery increased until I realized I was struggling to make myself get out of bed every morning. I had to force myself to get in the car to go to the office. On the drive to work I had to fight off irrational thoughts of wishing someone would hit me so I could see Jesus rather than face the day. Once I was in the office parking lot, I would often sit in the car for fifteen minutes or so and talk myself into opening the door. I got through many days by focusing on making it through one more hour. I'm not a super-spiritual guy, but I felt like I was engaged in hand-to-hand combat for my very soul.

The crazy thing for us is that as we discussed what I was going through, we both felt we were in the middle of God's will. The situation felt hopeless and full of God at the same time. The next step on our journey to understanding change was learning that you can do everything right, follow God's leading with all your heart, and still wind up in gut-wrenching misery. Fortunately, there is a biblical precedent for what we experienced.

Over and over we read about godly leaders making godly decisions and winding up in the deep weeds. Joseph refused Potiphar's wife and went from being a slave to being a prisoner. Hosea followed God's instructions and dealt with the pain of marital infidelity for the rest of his life. John the Baptist faithfully pointed the way to the coming Messiah only to be imprisoned and then beheaded for his unwavering faith.

After a year in California, Sherry accepted the CEO role at a Christian nonprofit called Mothers of Preschoolers International (MOPS). MOPS is headquartered in Denver, so once again we faced the prospect of starting over. By now, however, we understood the challenges of change, and we had healthy strategies in place to meet those challenges. Five years after moving to Denver we have again discovered a great church, great friends, and great ministry in one of the most beautiful places on earth.

Facing change in a healthy, God-honoring way is not a simple recipe for success. It produces something much deeper. Our brief time in California was incredibly valuable. I learned what it looks like to deal with real depression and how helpless we feel in the face of direct spiritual attack. We learned to lean into each other as we faced overwhelming challenges. We left California more committed to God, to ministry, and to each other than we'd ever been.

ANOTHER STORY OF CHANGE

Our dear friends Sibyl and Dick Towner, both former staff members of Willow Creek in Chicago, have experienced many seasons of change in their forty years of ministry together. Their journey has taken them on many turns and has led them to where they are today at the age of seventy-nine and seventy-five: codirectors of The Springs, a 150-acre retreat center in Indiana that serves those in Christian leadership, where they provide leadership training for teams and a quiet escape for pastors and their families. We asked Dick and Sibyl to share what they've learned about dealing with change along the way.

~

Well, of course, any vocational endeavor by a believer is ministry, but our vocational ministry within the church began for me (Dick) in 1976, when I was asked by our church in Cincinnati to become the executive pastor. Until then we were both convinced my lifetime ministry was in higher education, but God spoke very clearly that I was to join the staff of the church.

Since college Sibyl had been involved in summer camping and was asked in 1977 to start a camp for the church, which led to her becoming minister to families with children and director of summer ministries. We served together for almost thirteen years with eight other ministerial staff.

We had grown up in that church and felt that Cincinnati would always be our home. But in 1992 God spoke again and said I was to accept a position at Willow Creek after a consultation I had done for them. For the next nineteen years I served in several positions on both the church and the Willow Creek Association staffs, and while I was there I created the Good Sense Financial Ministry. Sibyl was also asked to help start a father-daughter camp, and as her gifts were recognized she served in several paid and unpaid staff positions during the nineteen years we were at Willow.

A season of change

In late 2009 we felt our time at Willow was complete and began plans to move back to Cincinnati. It was a difficult choice. We had developed deep friendships and had been used by God in so many ways. It was hard to say good-bye and hard to leave the beautiful home where we had invited so many in to share dinner and their lives with us. Due to the season we were in, we felt it was wise in this next move to rent rather than buy another home.

At Thanksgiving dinner in 2009 we told our family we would be returning to Cincinnati and would be living in an apartment. Our son, knowing my love of creation and the outdoors, said that if we were going to live in an apartment, there had better be somewhere in the country we could escape to on weekends or I would go stir crazy. That seemingly innocuous statement triggered a series of conversations between us and many yeses to God's nudging that led to our becoming directors of The Springs.

In our early years of marriage, fifty-plus years ago, we had briefly thought of leading a Christian camp. But in our wildest dreams we never thought we would be doing what we are doing today. Hardly a day goes by that we don't say to one another, "Can you believe we are here?" The process that led us here has been so unbelievable and so clearly God-led that our fears and worries were minimized, that is, we were confident we were to proceed, that it was the thing to do. But there were two big realities we had to face. First, in moving to The Springs (an hour outside of Cincinnati), we were going to be out in the boondocks, with no neighbors in sight and twenty-five minutes from the nearest small town with a grocery store. That would be a huge change and potential challenge, particularly for Sibyl, the consummate extrovert. Many of our friends were quite concerned for her.

The second reality was that the move was going to be expensive. The facilities were in need of major and costly repairs, there was very little guest use (meaning we had very little income), and we had to assume the six-figure debt of the ministry. At our stage in life it was daunting, but our life experience had made us very confident of God's provision.

Preparing for change

We believe we best prepare for change by being intentional about life and marriage along the way so as to be on firm ground when change comes. And we know it always will. Here are some things we have integrated into our daily lives. We selected as our family verse a short passage from 1 Thessalonians: "Rejoice always, pray continually, give thanks in all circumstances; for this is God's will for you in Christ Jesus" (5:16–18). And we have attempted to look at life's changes through the lens of those verses.

We remind ourselves of the memorable events of the past as we make changes. As we were leaving Willow after nineteen years, we went out for dinner and decided to see if we could recollect nineteen memorable occurrences, good or maybe difficult, in which God had shown up in those years. We closed down the restaurant with forty-seven items on our list.

A central practice throughout our marriage has been taking a two-or three-day time away once a quarter. During that time, we ask each other three questions:

1. How is our relationship doing?
2. How are the children doing?
3. What do the next three months on our calendars look like?

We often read a book together that touches on an area of needed or desired growth.

As our children were moving out on their own and we were at or near midlife, we took time individually and together to examine, reflect upon, and envision the changes that come with each new season.

We have attempted to stay in touch with those of the generation ahead of us as well as the generation behind us. We're convinced that intergenerational contact can be an important asset in dealing with change. In addition to being in traditional couples' small groups, we have frequently convened intergenerational small groups comprised of folks from all across the age spectrum, with children included. We have also enjoyed being the so-called elders in groups of young married couples.

While not a practice for everyone, we have opened our home to young people, usually just out of college, to live with us as extended family. That practice has drawn out the best in us as we attempted to model Christian life and family to them.

Neither of us ever envisioned retirement in the traditional sit-back-and-take-it-easy sense of the word. At our age we both hope to have five to ten more years as directors. Retirement is a relatively new phenomenon in human history, a form of social engineering enacted during the Great Depression to provide jobs for younger folks. Unfortunately it seems to have evolved into a commonly held belief that life after sixty-five (or before!) is meant to be one of leisure. With the insight and wisdom that life's experience has granted us, we believe we are in a position to be more effective than ever in serving others, and we believe that God desires that for all his children for as long as they have breath.

The advantage of age is being able to look back and see the hand of God. It's something to look forward to! Sibyl and I love being able to look back and exclaim, "If that hadn't happened way back then, then [that next thing] wouldn't have happened, and that wouldn't have led to this, and we wouldn't be who and where we are now! Wow! We get to see God's plan in retrospect and marvel at it all."

THE MASTERPIECE

I (Sherry) will never forget a conversation I had with Sibyl not long after we had moved to California. I was missing my friends. I felt alone. I knew Geoff wasn't happy and I wondered if we had moved away from God. Then my phone rang. I poured my heart out to Sibyl, telling her I didn't have a close friend within a thousand miles.

In a calm voice she said: "Well, what do you think God might be up to? You know that he sees you and knows you're there. Are you willing to be uncomfortable for a little while to wait on his plan?"

It wasn't what I expected, but Sibyl knew sympathy alone wasn't what I needed. I wanted someone to feel as sorry for me as I did. What Sibyl wanted was to change my gaze. She encouraged me to widen my lens and think about what God might have in store for tomorrow and to consider an even bigger picture. How might today fit into the path of my yesterdays and tomorrows. Sibyl knew we can't see God's masterpiece when we focus only on today's brushstroke.

Isn't that a great perspective on change? Knowing that even though change may not make sense at the time or even be comfortable, you can be confident that God has a plan and it's a good one.

I had felt overwhelmed when we moved to Houston, then Charleston, then California, and then Denver. I didn't know we would have incredible ministry adventures in Houston like planting a church in a challenging rural area or opportunities in Charleston to work in children's ministry at a fast-growing church and be part of a multisite movement that would forever change our ministry perspective. I didn't know these moves would be woven together by God's hand to form both of our kids' ministry paths. I didn't know we would experience loneliness in California like we had never experienced it before, but that it would refine us as a couple and draw us closer together. There was no way I could see how the experience in Denver as a new CEO would be the most challenging and growth-filled season of my life and that I'd be a better leader because of it. I couldn't see any of this at first. But now I see it. God's hand. His beautiful, all knowing, I-got-you-covered hand.

So how about you? Does this chapter find you in the midst of a season of change that is thrilling? confusing? even miserable? Perhaps the change was your choice, but it isn't working out like you planned. Maybe you are wondering if God is up to anything.

We encourage you to hold on. Have the courage to see today for what it really is: a brushstroke of God's mighty hand in the masterpiece that is your life.

TO TALK ABOUT

- Are you now experiencing a season of change that is hard on your marriage? How are you being proactive to talk about it and process it together?

- Is there a season of change that you know is coming? What steps will you take to make sure it's a healthy change?

- How do you personally process change? Now is a great time to talk to each other about your past experiences with change and how they affect how you face it today.

10

The Second Act

When we were teenagers in St. Louis, one of our favorite places to go on a date was the Municipal Opera Theater (known as the Muny), which was an eleven-thousand-seat outdoor amphitheater. Sherry loved Broadway musicals and I (Geoff) loved Sherry. (I also loved that the last nine rows were always free of charge.) Eventually I learned to love musicals as well.

Every musical follows the same formula. In act 1 you are introduced to the characters and the world they inhabit. The plot is always based on changing relationships among the characters, such as the budding romance in *The Sound of Music* between Maria and the captain and the adoption of Cosette by Jean Valjean in *Les Misérables*. There is always a crisis at some point toward the end of act 1, and in both *The Sound of Music* and *Les Misérables*, the crisis is an impending war. By intermission, if the cast has done its job, you are so engaged in the relationships you have to stay to discover how the crisis will be resolved. (Unless you are watching *Oklahoma!*, in which case you are just begging for it to end.) Act 2 is all about resolving the crisis set up in act 1. The von Trapps' escape to Austria, Cosette and her true love Marius are finally united, Annie gets her gun (actually we have no idea—we haven't seen *Annie Get Your Gun*).

Marriage and ministry follow a similar pattern to musicals. Act 1 is about establishing the cast of characters and the world you live in. You meet your spouse, you discover your calling, and you start your family. The focus of act 1 is about tasks and results. Your days are ordered around getting the kids to school, planning events at church, attending sporting events and recitals, and connecting with leaders at the church. There is always more to do than could possibly be accomplished in a day, so to borrow a phrase from Andy Stanley, you choose to cheat. You take some time from family and use it at church or you take time away from ministry to focus on your family. The pressure of time, resources, and relationship is nonstop.

Knowing how act 1 is going seems fairly straightforward. How are the kids doing in school? Does your son have friends? Did your daughter make the traveling squad? How is attendance at church? What about offerings? Are we baptizing more people this year than we did last? Did we bring back the same number of teenagers as we took to summer camp? Regardless of how the numbers look, however, there are always crises during act 1.

For us, one of the most challenging crises we faced was the marriage ditch we experienced (see chapter 4). For some couples, one of the kids goes off the rails, others face a ministry crisis, and the rest struggle with their finances. Everyone faces the brink of disaster. Sadly, not all ministry couples have an act 2. Unlike a scripted musical, a moral failure, divorce, or death may cut the story short. Most of us, however, will eventually deal with the very different reality of act 2.

Through our years of ministry, we have always noticed other couples in ministry who do it well, meaning they are able to not take themselves too seriously, to feel at home in their skin, and bring you along in their comfortableness when you sit at their table for dinner. Jerry and Lana McSwain served alongside us at Seacoast, and they are one of those couples. They've been married for forty-six years, and for more than twenty years they've served in ministry together vocationally and as volunteers. They are the proud parents of two adult children and even prouder grandparents of five, ranging in age from preschool to middle school. One of the traits we admire most about Jerry and Lana is their ability to relax and have fun, enjoying their ministry and each other even in the midst of pressure. As we have watched them redefine themselves in their second act, we have thought we would want to be like them, so we asked them to share their story.

—

When I (Jerry) left a staff position as pastor at Seacoast Church in Mount Pleasant, we honestly weren't sure what our next role would be. We knew God was calling us to a new chapter of leadership, but we weren't sure what it looked like. At Seacoast, Lana and I initially were volunteer small-group leaders, which ultimately led to my joining the staff and leading in several areas, including marriage and small groups. Lana taught in the public schools, but she was right by my side in every ministry opportunity.

As we've stepped into our second act, it looks different than it has in the past. We spend our summers in Montana, serving in New Frontier Ministries, a discipleship ministry for fathers and sons. During the rest of the year we're active in training high-capacity leaders in implementing and leading discipleship and missional groups in their communities and churches. We also have the honor of mentoring several pastors and building relationships of encouragement with church planters across the country.

Lana and I would characterize this season as one of margin and adventure, with more time to share and work together than ever before. It's sometimes hard for our adult children to understand and for us to know when we need to be available to their families and, honestly, when we can just take a pass. We love spending our summers in Montana (I used to be a forest ranger), but it's a huge commitment away from our family. There always seems to be an increasingly weighty pressure of a limited window of time we will have to pour into our grandkids and also maintain a ministry that involves extensive travel. We're smart enough to know that our grandkids will one day be too busy for us, but we also know that Jesus has invited us into the incredible things he is doing, and we don't want to miss any of it. The empty-nest part of our second half is both easier and harder at the same time. We don't have young children in the house anymore, which brings freedom, but as our two adult children have established their families and spread out, we've come to realize we can't be a part of every special occasion or holiday. We constantly find ourselves seeking a sane balance between family and calling, similar to when our kids were younger, but in a new way.

Our second act has reframed what our picture of ministry success looks like. When I was on staff at a local church, the pressure of the immediate was always present and never satisfied. Now that Lana and I get to build what our ministry looks like, we've both been able to truly clarify our calling to equip disciples who equip disciples. We have the freedom to select who we pour into, weeding out those who really aren't that interested. We've come to realize that in doing less we're actually producing more. Success for us now is walking with a clear focus on God's voice and nothing else. We know we're not doing it perfectly, but our work is incredibly satisfying. The "person of peace" principle from Luke 10:5–7 has been incredibly liberating for us.

As we think about what keeps our marriage vital in this season, the thing we fight for most is healthy rhythms. Our perspective has changed. We work from our rest, not rest from our work. The summer offers a unique rhythm as we work one week and take the next week off. We love working together, and ministry enriches our lives, drawing us closer. We read posts and books, share material that catches our attention, and have time to discuss and listen to each other's insights. Lana has a keen ability to organize information and sequence it properly, which I utilize often. Given that I am the world's worst speller, she proofs most of what I write and is kind enough to allow me to make comments on her writing. We also have given each other permission to hold the other accountable, especially regarding our attitudes. We pray for each other and over each other regularly.

Between Christmas and New Year's, we both independently spend time seeking what God might be saying to us for the coming year. Once we both have an answer, we compare notes and put the biggest occasions on our calendar. Each of us has opportunities that we pursue independently. And most evenings over dinner we catch each other up on whatever the day has brought. Adventure is a key value that we pursue and one that enriches our lives, so we don't shy away from travel and new opportunities. At the same time, we have also been fighting for simplicity in our lives, especially regarding relationships and material things. This has not come easily, but we are leaning into it.

In the past the default has usually been for me (Jerry) to take the lead in our ministry; however, as I have watched Lana grow and develop, I realize that she is much better at many, if not most, of the ministry opportunities we have. Her discernment is invaluable and I seldom make a move without running it by her. This hasn't come easily for either of us, but we try to be intentional and encourage each other at every opportunity, and we use each other as a sounding board. Without a doubt, it has become crystal clear to me that we are better together now more than ever!

THE SECOND ACT IS ABOUT RELATIONSHIPS

We love how Jerry and Lana have discovered ministry beyond the weekend pressure. We're discovering that act 2 is also more about relationships than outcomes in our lives. The relational work we did, or didn't do, in act 1 is now bearing fruit. After many years of influencing or controlling every decision my kids made, I'm now on the sidelines, cheering them on. They ask for advice, but the decisions they make are theirs. I'm no longer responsible for the results of those decisions. I find that my emphasis in ministry has shifted as well. For the first three decades of ministry it was about the numbers. I expected to see larger attendance this year than last. If we had ten volunteers last month, I hoped to see fifteen this month. I still care about numbers, but I'm no longer as invested in numbers as I am in the lives those numbers represent.

I was talking to a megachurch pastor recently who is in the second act of his life. He leads a church that has posted some amazing numbers for many years, but he said another big Christmas Eve or another big Easter no longer motivates him. He is thinking about the lives that are impacted not just by his church but by the churches they have planted and the missions they support around the world. It is more about relational influence than numbers on a spreadsheet.

REDISCOVER YOUR RELATIONSHIP WITH GOD

In the relative quiet of act 2 we're rediscovering our relationships with God. In act 1, I (Geoff) often allowed the drive of ministry and family to push God to a side room of my heart. I continued to read my Bible and to journal, but I didn't take the time to pay attention to the quiet rhythm of my soul.

Now that the drive is changing, I am finding new ways to listen to God's voice. A scripture that speaks loudly to me in the quiet comes from Isaiah:

> Who among you fears the LORD
>   and obeys the word of his servant?
> Let the one who walks in the dark,
>   who has no light,
> trust in the name of the LORD
>   and rely on their God.
> But now, all you who light fires
>   and provide yourselves with flaming torches,
> go, walk in the light of your fires
>   and of the torches you have set ablaze.
> This is what you shall receive from my hand:
>   You will lie down in torment.

(50:10–11)

My response to darkness in act 1 was to light my own light. I didn't understand the power of quiet and solitude, waiting patiently for God to act. Looking back, I realize many of the crises in my act 1 were created by this inability to be comfortable in the darkness, to realize that when there's not a clear direction it's okay to wait. Part of the moves we dealt with in chapter 9 came out of this fire-lighting tendency. When I felt a restlessness or boredom, I decided it was time to move on. But I am learning that in the darkness, when the next move isn't obvious, God is often calling me to sit, to listen, and to wait for his voice.

One of the things I love about act 2 is the quiet of the mornings. When the children were home, the buzz in the house started the minute they got up. They had to be dressed, fed, and out the door or they'd be late for school. Someone was either missing a shoe, forgot they were supposed to bring breakfast for the entire fourth grade, or needed their uniform washed almost every day of the week. But mornings now are for solitude. I especially love snowy mornings when a fire is going, the coffee is on, and the house is silent. It is a time to read, to pray, and to listen. I miss the kids, but I love the margin to connect with God before the whirlwind begins.

REKINDLE THE RELATIONSHIP
WITH YOUR SPOUSE

Sherry and I are finding the second act to be the richest season in our marriage. We miss the kids, but we love the fact that any night can be date night. Sometimes in the middle of the week we decide to leave work early and see a matinee. On Saturdays we often jump into the Jeep and head to the mountains with no destination in mind. It's amazing how freeing it is not to have anyone asking where we are going or when we will get there. We love to travel, and now we get to travel together to some of the most amazing places on the planet. In fact, I'm writing this on a plane after a few days on the Amalfi Coast of Italy. Without the pressure of ball games and recitals, we have time to sit and talk about the really important things. The other night we sat at the dinner table for two and a half hours talking about the kids, the future, our sex life, and our connection with God. That never happened when the kids lived at home. Now it happens once or twice a week.

One of the things we have found invaluable in rekindling our relationship in act 2 is incorporating some rituals in our daily lives. We briefly touched on some of these rituals in chapter 5, but we wanted to share a little more context here.

The first ritual starts almost every day. In the morning, before either of us leaves the house, we take a few minutes to ask two questions:

1. What is your day like?
2. How can I pray for you today?

We briefly talk through our schedules, highlight areas where prayer would be appreciated, and then take turns praying for each other.

A second ritual we've incorporated is over our evening meal at home. We take turns cooking a simple meal that we can eat together at the kitchen table. We light a candle to represent God's presence with us. When we are done eating, we ask, "Where did you see God at work today?" We finish by reading and discussing a brief devotional and sharing a prayer together.

A third ritual we've incorporated is romance night. When the kids were home, intimacy was always a challenge. Juggling ministry, work, multiple schedules, and maintaining a household left little room to enjoy God's gift of sex. After the kids moved out, we had more time, but we still struggled to prioritize this beautiful but sometimes challenging area of married life. Recently we've begun designating certain nights as romance nights. This means we will spend the entire evening focusing on each other. No television. No phones. No computers. Because we have the house to ourselves we often stay home on romance night and spend the entire evening rekindling the intimacy God intended for marriage. Act 2 is turning out to be a lot of fun.

REDEFINE YOUR RELATIONSHIP WITH YOUR KIDS

Some friends who teach parenting classes define the stages of parenting as teacher, coach, and cheerleader. You begin by teaching your children everything they need to know to survive in life. Soon you are coaching them from the sidelines as they make their own mistakes. Eventually you are cheering them on as they figure things out on their own. Looking back from the other side, it is amazing how quickly each stage fades into the next, and the speed at which it all disappears takes your breath away. If you still have kids in diapers, I know it's hard to believe, but it will seem like only days between kindergarten and college.

Now that our kids have moved out and have lives of their own, we are discovering a fourth stage of parenting: friend. We love spending time with our kids and their friends and families. It is fascinating to get their take on our rapidly changing world. They have a depth and breadth of knowledge that amazes me. I love listening to our son share the latest topic he's researching or hearing about a cause my daughter is passionate about. There are many areas in which we now go to our kids for advice, and they continue to come to us as well. We miss the days of games and graduations, but we would never trade the richness of friendship for the chance to go back.

REFOCUS ON RELATIONSHIPS IN MINISTRY

The biggest joy in ministry in the second act is seeing younger leaders succeed, young leaders like some of those we heard from earlier in the book, each of whom we've had the honor of sowing into their lives. In act 2 the competitive side of ministry fades, and what remains are the relationships we build. It is significant that Jesus' last night, before being arrested, was spent not teaching a huge audience, but at a quiet dinner with friends. The second act gives us the time and margin to invest in other ministries. I love what Bob Buford, founder of Leadership Network and HalfTime Institute, says about the second act of ministry: "Our fruit grows on other people's trees."

As we dream about the rest of act 2, we are focused on investing in tomorrow. How can we use the lessons we've learned in thirty-plus years of ministry to help those who are just entering the journey to succeed? It is a season of going from maestro to mentor, moving from being the show to providing the platform. It is one of the most rewarding seasons of ministries we've experienced.

TO TALK ABOUT

- What part of the second act of ministry and life together sounds appealing to you? What sounds scary?

- How can you prepare today for a great second act?

- Who do you know would be a great mentor in navigating the second act successfully? How can you begin intentionally learning from them?

Conclusion:

~

What We Wish for You

As we were in the middle stages of writing this book, Sherry started experiencing symptoms that led to a doctor's appointment. We assumed she'd be given a prescription and everything would be okay. Instead, the doctor expressed serious concern. She ordered a series of tests, and then she said they needed to do a biopsy. For the first time in our marriage the word *cancer* was on the table. We were terrified that the second act of our marriage, the chapter after the kids were on their own and we were no longer driven to expand ministry, would be cut short. The doctor said it would be several days before the test results would come back, days that would prove to be the longest of our lives.

We decided to take our little travel trailer to our favorite spot in the mountains and spend some time enjoying the beauty of the Rockies together. As we sat by the campfire we talked again of all God had accomplished in and through us. We laughed about the silly things our grandkids said the last time we were together. We reminded ourselves how proud we are of our children and the leaders they've become. And we reminisced about the incredible adventure we've been on for over thirty years together. We were terrified of what the future might hold, but as we sat in the fading sunset on that clear, crisp mountain evening beside a crackling fire, we were so thankful for all that had come before. If this was indeed the beginning of the end, we were ready to face whatever might come—together.

Wherever you are on your journey together, we want to leave you with a few final pieces of advice.

1. *Focus on relationships*: There will come a day when weekend attendance, offerings, and even baptisms will seem unimportant. All the things you keep track of in ministry will fade, and only the relationships you've invested in will make a difference. Focus today on your relationship with God and the state of your soul. Soul care isn't just for contemplatives

who write in journals and go on retreats. Soul care is what keeps you connected to God when everything else falls apart.

Focus on your relationship with your spouse. Initiate difficult conversations about shame, sex, fear, and all the stuff you don't want to talk about but know you have to. Go see a counselor. Bribe your parents to take the kids for the weekend. Sell your car and take your wife to Italy.

Focus on your relationship with your kids. Tell your kids you love them, and then show them by making them a higher priority than the church. Not just their ball games, but them. Invest the next few years in the things that matter and invest in tomorrow today. Find another married couple to pour your life into. Find out where the other pastors in town are struggling and help them. Become a mentor to a younger leader today and cheer for them as their ministry influence surpasses yours.

2. *Let go of worry*: Remember the nights you spend worrying if a particular family is going to quit your church? Whether the giving campaign is going to bring in *any* money at all? What will happen if your son continues to date *that* girl? We know how you feel. If worry were an Olympic sport, we'd win the gold medal in the pairs competition.

In *The Essence of Success*, Earl Nightingale says only 8 percent of what we worry about could actually happen.[4] That means we spend 92 percent of our worry time worrying about things that are impossible and making ourselves miserable for no reason. We want to encourage you to let it go. Say so long to the sweaty moments of panic over what's not going to happen and focus your gaze on the precious people in your house whom God allows you to live life with. Sometimes you have to wait until they are asleep to see how special they are, but that's okay. We've paid the dumb tax on worry. It does no good, and it wastes your precious moments you have together.

3. *Let go of expectations*: Author Lisa Kleypas observed: "We are our own worst enemy. If we can learn to stop expecting impossible perfection, in ourselves and others, we may just find the happiness that has always eluded us."[5]

For years, we've each battled unrealistic expectations in many areas. Our church needed to keep growing. We needed to get the next promotion. Our kids not only needed to graduate but also to get a college scholarship. We felt the need to prove ourselves, not just to others, but to each other. After all, we have potential and we need to fulfill it. We have a calling and we need to be faithful to it. God has given us talent and skills and we better figure out how to use them.

Can you relate?

Here's what we're learning. God has certainly placed a calling on our lives, but it's not a call to our definition of success. It's to have a deep relationship with him, to sit in his gaze and hear his voice whispering: *I am with you wherever you go. I am mighty to save you. I take great delight in you and will quiet you with my love. I will rejoice over you with singing* (cf. Zeph. 3:17).

But doesn't it feel like this is only true if we're trying hard? If our church is big enough? If our family looks like we think it should? If other people call us a success?

Let it go. Lay down the disappointment that keeps you from laughing with your kids until soda spurts out your nose. Reclaim your lighthearted self that has been buried so deep. Ignore the fact that you don't have any rhythm—dance anyway. Hide around the corner from your spouse and jump out unexpectedly. (Sherry thinks this is hilarious. Geoff, not so much.)

As we conclude *Together*, we hope a few of our stories have made you chuckle, but we also hope you've had moments of "me too" when our story resonated with yours. We hope you've had nights together when something we wrote sparked a deep conversation and created the space to talk about things you never have before.

Ministry is fun. Your marriage is worth it. Fight for both.

We began by saying we want this book to feel like a conversation over a cup of coffee and a really good piece of pie. Now, if you would, picture us looking you in the eye and giving you a challenge.

Wherever your marriage is right now, it can get better. You have no idea what God has around the next corner. If you give up now, you won't ever see it. If you are in a desperate or distant place, hold on. If life is good, it can get even *gooder* (we have special permission from one of our editors to use that word).

We love to say this because it's the truth and we are living proof. If we had given up in chapter 4 there never would have been a second act to write about in chapter 10. Our second act has been so worth it. We've learned how to pray together, how to have fun together, how to make love to each other. It has taken more than thirty years of marriage to get here. It's okay. You can call us slow.

A few days after our camping trip, the doctor called with the test results. The tumor was benign. Sherry is going to be fine. You can only understand our relief if you've experienced a similar scare. We've laughed, we've cried, and we've thanked God for another chance to finish well. We are going to play it for all we're worth. We hope you will as well.

Acknowledgments

~

We want to thank our friends at Leadership Network, who have encouraged us in so many ways through the years, including saying, "We really think you should write a book together." Much to our surprise we actually wrote the book, and we remained friends in the process.

We also want to thank the staff at Thomas Nelson, who have flexed and flexed again to accommodate the world's worst procrastinators. We promise we'll hit the next deadline.

And finally we want to thank the incredible couples in ministry, who shared their stories with us. We are grateful. It's our joy to call you our friends and to experience how God is working in your marriages and ministries.

Notes

~

1. Gordon MacDonald, "God's Calling Plan," *Christianity Today* (Fall 2003). http://www.christianitytoday.com/pastors/2003/fall/3.35.html.
2. Eric Jackson, "The Top Ten Lessons Steve Jobs Taught Us," *Forbes* (5 October 2011), https://www.forbes.com/sites/ericjackson/2011/10/05/the-top-ten-lessons-steve-jobs-taught-us/#11b810107bfb.
3. Reggie Joiner and Carey Nieuwhof, *Parenting Beyond Your Capacity: Connect Your Family to a Wider Community* (Colorado Springs: David C. Cook, 2010, 2015), 75.
4. Earl Nightingale, *The Essence of Success* (New York: Beta Nu Publishing, 2007).
5. Lisa Kleypas, *Love in the Afternoon* (New York: St. Martins Press, 2010), 321.

About the Authors

Geoff and Sherry Surratt have served in ministry, both individually and together, for more than thirty-five years. Sherry has been a classroom teacher, a children's ministry pastor, a church consultant, as well as CEO of Mothers of Preschoolers (MOPS International). She is currently the Executive Director of Parenting Strategy at the Rethink Group.

Geoff has served churches in a variety of roles, including student pastor, executive pastor, and lead pastor, as well as consulting with church leaders around the world.

Geoff and Sherry have written several books individually, including *Ten Stupid Things That Keep Churches from Growing*, *The Multisite Church Revolution*, *Brave Mom*, and

Just Lead! A No Whining, No Complaining, No Nonsense Practical Guide for Women Leaders in the Church. They live just outside of Denver, Colorado, and love hanging out with their kids and grandkids.

MinistryTogether

Our mission at MinistryTogether is to help you reach your full potential as a person, as a leader and as an organization. With over 30 years of experience helping leaders, churches and non-profits grow, let's talk about how MinistryTogether can come alongside you.

MINISTRYTOGETHER OFFERS

Practical resources ✳ Collaborative learning experiences

Strategic planning ✳ Ministry coaching

Marriage retreats ✳ Leadership training

MINISTRYTOGETHER.COM

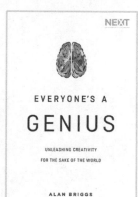

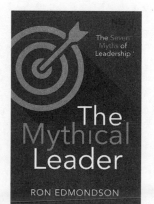